City Breaks
in
Florence

REG BUTLER

In Association with

THOMSON HOLIDAYS

SETTLE PRESS

Text © 1994 Reg Butler

First published by Settle Press
10 Boyne Terrace Mews
London W11 3LR

ISBN (Paperback) 1 872876 26 9

Printed by Villiers Publications
19 Sylvan Avenue
London N3 2LE
Maps by courtesy of the Italian State Tourist Office

Foreword

As Britain's leading short breaks specialist, we recognise the need for detailed information and guidance for CityBreak travellers. But much more is required than just a listing of museums and their opening times. For a few days, the CityBreak visitor wants to experience the local continental lifestyle.

We are therefore very pleased to work with Reg Butler and Settle Press on this latest addition to the CityBreak series of pocket guide-books.

Reg Butler has had considerably experience of the great Italian cities. As a young courier, he conducted ten full seasons of grand European tours, with regular visits to Venice, Florence and Rome. Since then he has returned many times to Italy, writing travel articles for British and American newspapers and magazines.

For this book Reg Butler has collaborated closely with our resident Thomson staff, who have year-round experience of helping visitors enjoy these cities. We're sure you'll find this book invaluable in planning how to make best personal use of your time.

As well as CityBreaks in Rome, Florence and Venice, other books in the series cover Paris, Amsterdam, Vienna, Salzburg, Budapest and Prague. Thomson also operate to many other world cities from departure points across the UK.

THOMSON CITYBREAKS

Contents

Chapter One

Romantic Florence

Florence is a remarkable city, with art treasures that are unparalleled anywhere in the world. It's a prosperous and bustling city of elegance and refinement – reflected in its 20th-century reputation for fashion, craftsmanship, antiques and culture. As the cradle of the Renaissance, the Tuscan capital is packed with the finest paintings and sculptures of that extraordinary 150-year period from 1400 to 1550 when Florence led a re-birth of European civilisation.

Let's just mention a few names of former residents who brought fame to Florence: Petrarch, Dante and Boccaccio, among the writers and poets; Giotto, Leonardo, Michelangelo and Botticelli among the dozens of world-class painters; Machiavelli among the political thinkers; three centuries of the Medici family. The Tuscan dialect which they all spoke became today's purest textbook Italian, closest to the original Latin.

In its setting amid hills on the banks of River Arno, Florence has preserved her medieval and Renaissance heritage of great churches, palaces, statues and bridges. Most of those great names from the past could easily find their way around the present-day centre of Florence.

Finance for this rich golden age came from banking, and the wool and silk trade. In the 1420's, Florence had 72 operating banks which lent money and peddled influence throughout Italy and elsewhere in Europe. The enormous banking and merchant profits were ploughed into great mansions, furnished with luxury.

The Medici heritage

The dominant Medici family – first Giovanni (1360-1429) who founded the family fortune; then his son Cosimo the Elder (1389-1464) who became absolute ruler of the Florentine Republic; then a long line of successors – built great palaces and public monuments, and lavished money on the promotion of letters and the arts. The Medici name was everywhere.

The cultural tradition persisted. During the great days of the Grand Tour, the aristocratic travellers of the 18th and 19th centuries always included a prolonged stop in Florence, to absorb something of the city's artistic riches.

This was an essential part of a wealthy young man's education. A rich man's son would develop a taste for paintings, sculpture and architecture; pick up some basic languages; learn something of history, cultivate an ear for good music, and a taste for something more than English roast beef.

There was ample light relief on the Grand Tour: the pleasure of conversation with other grand travellers; going to masked balls and carnivals; flirting with the local girls; drinking the wines.

Especially from the early 19th century, Florence became a congenial 'paradise of exiles' – from Shelley and Dostoevsky to Elizabeth Barrett Browning, Mark Twain, Henry James and D.H. Lawrence. Numerous painters made the pilgrimage to Florence, to gain added insight into the techniques of the great Renaissance masters.

Today, few people can afford a year or two's *time* for an Italian Grand Tour. But the ease of modern air travel has brought Florence within easy reach of a long weekend citybreak. In three or four days, the 20th-century traveller can skim the sightseeing cream of the world's greatest collections of Renaissance painting and sculpture.

On a one-week trip, there's ample scope for more in-depth cultivation of a particular interest, or for exploring other towns and the surrounding countryside on day excursions; or for combining Florence in a two-centre arrangement with Venice or Rome.

Beyond the galleries

A visit to Florence is a journey into the past, greatly enlivened by the present. Its full appeal is not buried in museums. Few other cities have such magnificent antique stores, alternating with workshops of a dozen different living crafts: leather and raffia work, gold and silver jewellery, art reproductions, mosaics and exquisite embroidery.

Florence can rank among the top rivals to Paris for high fashion, glittering with great names but still leaving room for hundreds of small boutiques to make a decent living.

Of course Florence is heaven for art-lovers. A seven-day citybreak can be filled with galleries every day, an embarrassment of artistic riches. Even then, it's impossible to do more than lightly skim the surface of these great collections.

For the less dedicated, two or three days is sufficient for Basic Florence. Don't wear yourself out with too many museums! Enjoy the leisured delights of the good Italian wine and cuisine, the pleasure of watching the passing scene from a pavement café, or taking an evening stroll around the Piazza della Signoria and across the Ponte Vecchio. Let yourself be carried away by the sheer romance of Florence and the Florentine life-style.

Above all, make time to use Florence as a touring base to see some of the landscapes which inspired the great Renaissance painters.

Take an afternoon excursion into the beautiful countryside of Tuscany, with its gently rolling hills, farmhouses, olive groves and cypress trees. There are famous spas to visit, such as Montecatini and Bagni di Lucca. You should definitely make time for sightseeing in Pisa, Siena or the fabulous medieval walled city of San Gimignano.

Certainly there's much more to a citybreak in Florence than trudging around the galleries! All that sensuous beauty could make it a great place for a honeymoon or a long romantic weekend.

Chapter Two

Arrival in Florence

2.1 Which season?

When to visit Florence? For a dedicated art lover who likes to savour paintings in tranquility, it's seriously worth considering Florence in winter, with the eveningtime bonus of classical concerts or opera.

Otherwise, Florence is a city for all seasons. Spring or autumn are idyllic seasons for enjoyment of Florence and the surrounding countryside.

Especially at Easter, the big rush starts. In the hotter summer months, many sightseers adopt the good Italian tradition of an afternoon siesta. It's not a 'waste' of time. You are then refreshed for a cooler return to the sightseeing circuits, followed by the tranquil pleasures of open-air dining, or watching the world go by from pavement cafés.

The July-August climate can be hot and sticky, but Florence is then at its liveliest with international visitors. During high summer you can find cooler evenings by attending the summer festival of music, ballet and drama at Fiesole – the hilltop location a few miles outside Florence.

Among the other annual events, high fashion shows – Italian and international – are held in March and October at the Pitti Palace. On Easter Day there's midday mass and fireworks – 'Explosion of the Cart' (*Scoppio del Carro*) – at the Duomo.

If you're a soccer fan, here's something different: a 16th-century game of football, in medieval costume and no holds barred, in Piazza della Signoria on June 24 and 28.

2.2 Flying in to Florence

The international airport serving Florence is Pisa, 50 miles west. Most visitors on charter flights from Gatwick or Manchester usually have a transfer included to their chosen hotel.

Otherwise, go-it-alone travellers will find the handiest transport into Florence is by rail. A train at the airport railway station takes you direct to Stazione Santa Maria di Novella Firenze (Florence Station, for short). The journey time is one hour.

A useful sentence is "A che ora parte il treno per Firenze?" – "What time does the train leave for Florence?"

There is a taxi rank beside the station, on Piazza Adua. The price is metered, with a supplement of 500 lire per suitcase.

That same main railway station is used by travellers on two-centre holidays, linking Florence with either Rome or Venice.

On the return journey to Pisa airport, note that certain trains run directly to Pisa airport terminal, 'aeroporto'. Be careful not to get off by mistake at the previous stop, which is Pisa Centrale. It's another five minutes' train ride to the airport.

2.3 Your hotel

Hotels in Florence tend to be either the large modern variety, or the small family pensione style, full of local character.

Check-in: Normal check-in and check-out time is midday. If you arrive before noon, you may check in and leave luggage with reception until your room is free. If your final departure is after midday, pack bags before going out for the morning and leave them in the left-luggage room.

Getting in late: Some hotels lock their doors after midnight. If you plan to be out late, advise the concierge beforehand, just to be sure that a night porter can let you in!

Electricity: Italian electricity is 220 volts. Plugs are generally Continental-style two-pin. Pack a plug adaptor if you expect to use your own electric gadgets.

Lighting: Hotel corridors sometimes have a time switch for the lights, long enough to unlock your door. Look for a small orange light and press the button.

Water taps: 'C' stands for *caldo*, meaning hot; 'F' is *freddo*, meaning cold.

Breakfast: Italian breakfasts are modest Continental – bread or rolls, jam or marmalade, a scraping of butter, and tea or coffee. Normally it's served early, available between 7.30 and 9.30.

Tipping: Around 500 lire per case is usual for porters. Chambermaids will appreciate the lire you leave for them in the bedroom at the end of your stay.

2.4 Orientation and transport

The historic centre of Florence is very compact, and you can easily visit most of the principal sites on foot. Indeed, most of the great highlights are inside a central pedestrian zone, within a brief stroll of Piazza della Signoria.

Take a few minutes to study the map. From the Central Railway Station, the heart of Florence is tightly packed into a semi-circle that reaches to the River Arno.

A ring of boulevards called the Viali marks the boundaries of the original walled city. Just about everything worth seeing north of the Arno is contained within that ring-road.

The most important bridge on the sightseeing circuit is Ponte Vecchio, which is the shortest route between the Uffizi Gallery and Pitti Palace on the south side of the River Arno.

Note the location of the other main sites – the Cathedral which has a direct link to Piazza della Signoria along Via dei Calzaìuoli and thence to Piazza Santa Croce – and you have the orientation problem licked.

Depending on location of your hotel, you may need public transport into the centre: that is, to Stazione Centrale, the railway station. Otherwise, you'll hardly ever have any use of public transport, except maybe an occasional taxi or out-of-town bus.

Buses (autobus)

Florence is well served by a comprehensive bus network. Buy tickets at A.T.A.F. kiosks or at bars or tobacconists (*tabaccaio*). Cost is 1,200 lire for each journey. Save time and money by buying a block of 4, 8 or 12 tickets at once. When you board the bus – at the back – stamp your ticket in the red machine.

There's a Bus Information Office – A.T.A.F. – at 57r Piazza del Duomo, where you can get a useful free bus map. Tel: 21 23 01.

Useful bus routes:

No. 7 – to Fiesole
No. 13 – to Piazza Michelangelo
No. 16 – from Vittorio Veneto to the centre (Hotel Michelangelo).

Taxis

Taxis may be hailed in the street, but can be elusive. Empty cabs which ignore you are often on a call. Go to the nearest main square and wait hopefully at the taxi stand. From a hotel or restaurant, the concierge or cashier can phone for a radio-cab. The magic phone numbers are 4390 or 4798. The meter starts working from when the driver is called.

Fares are metered, and there are supplements for suitcases (500 lire each); Sunday 1,000 lire; and 1,000 lire extra after 10 p.m. Tipping is about 10%.

N.B. If you have any doubts about your taxi, note down the licence number. Avoid using drivers who approach you, as they are usually unofficial, with no meters, and can scalp you on fares.

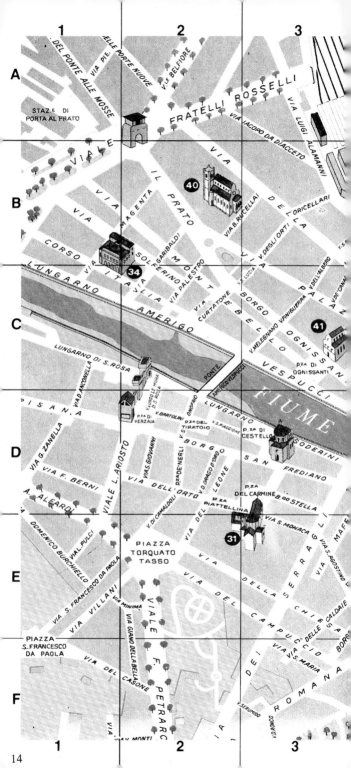

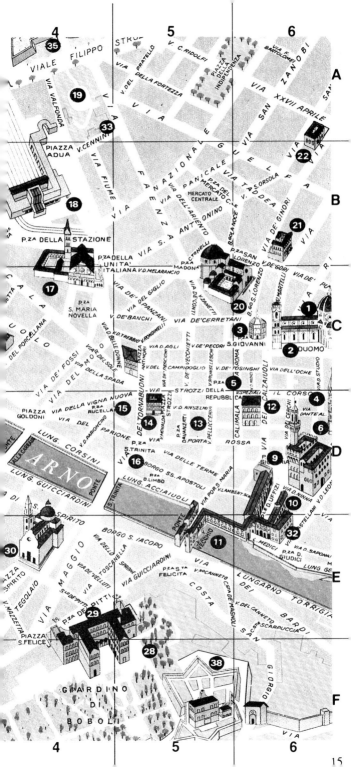

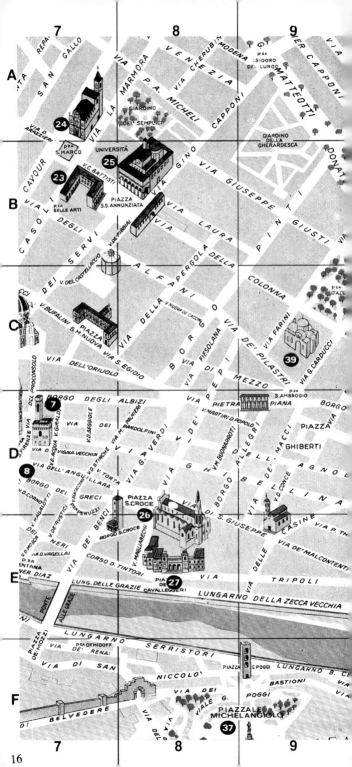

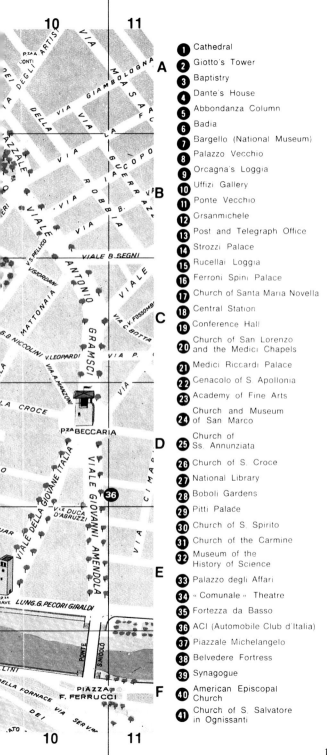

1. Cathedral
2. Giotto's Tower
3. Baptistry
4. Dante's House
5. Abbondanza Column
6. Badia
7. Bargello (National Museum)
8. Palazzo Vecchio
9. Orcagna's Loggia
10. Uffizi Gallery
11. Ponte Vecchio
12. Orsanmichele
13. Post and Telegraph Office
14. Strozzi Palace
15. Rucellai Loggia
16. Ferroni Spini Palace
17. Church of Santa Maria Novella
18. Central Station
19. Conference Hall
20. Church of San Lorenzo and the Medici Chapels
21. Medici Riccardi Palace
22. Cenacolo of S. Apollonia
23. Academy of Fine Arts
24. Church and Museum of San Marco
25. Church of Ss. Annunziata
26. Church of S. Croce
27. National Library
28. Boboli Gardens
29. Pitti Palace
30. Church of S. Spirito
31. Church of the Carmine
32. Museum of the History of Science
33. Palazzo degli Affari
34. « Comunale » Theatre
35. Fortezza da Basso
36. ACI (Automobile Club d'Italia)
37. Piazzale Michelangelo
38. Belvedere Fortress
39. Synagogue
40. American Episcopal Church
41. Church of S. Salvatore in Ognissanti

17

Chapter Three

Plan your sightseeing

3.1 Essential Florence

If you go overboard on art appreciation, then Florence will keep you going for months with its great galleries and churches. Otherwise, for the short-time visitor, here's a basic check-list for enjoyment of a brief stay.

• Feast your eyes in the Pitti Palace, followed by a stroll through the Boboli Gardens.
• On another day, visit Rooms 7-15 on second floor of the Uffizi Gallery.
• Explore the Cathedral – Duomo – and the adjoining buildings.
• Stroll around floodlit Florence, and pause for lengthy refreshment at an outdoor café.
• Shop-gaze for gold across Ponte Vecchio; or listen to street musicians there, at night.
• Break for classical music at the Teatro Comunale or elsewhere, according to seasonal programme.
• Watch craftsmen in workshops around Piazza S. Croce – leather, silverware, mosaics – and visit the Franciscan church.
• Eat a Florentine beefsteak – bistecca alla Fiorentina – with a bottle of Chianti classico.
• Visit the hill town of Fiesole by night, for summertime musical events in the Roman Theatre.
• Spare an afternoon for a Pisa excursion, to check how the Leaning Tower is making out.

Most of Basic Florence is covered by the standard City Tour offered by local travel agencies. It's better to take that half-day orientation tour, rather than fumbling around on your own and possibly missing some of the great highlights. These tours normally visit the Piazza della Signoria; either the Pitti Palace or the Uffizi; the Cathedral area; the Accademia, mainly to see Michelangelo's *David*; Ponte Vecchio; Piazza Santa Croce; and the hilltop view of Florence from Piazzale Michelangelo.

3.2 Sunday in Florence

There's plenty doing in Florence on a Sunday. Virtually all the museums and galleries are open at least until lunch-time. With shops and businesses closed, traffic is much less intense. Pedestrians can walk without being fumigated. Photographers can step into the road for that better-composed picture, without being mown down by a passing Fiat.

However, if you're at a loose end, here are some suggestions:

Excursions
Why not sit back, and take a trip? Excursions available on a Sunday include (a) the standard City Tour, (b) half-day to Pisa, or (c) a full day to Siena. Your travel-agency representative can make reservations, or suggest other alternatives.

Shops & Markets
Shops are closed, but the Straw Market on Piazza dei Ciompi is in full swing.

Museums & Galleries
Some charge a reduced entrance fee on Sundays. See Chapter 7 for further details.

Church Services
Mass in English is held at Santa Maria del Fiore (Duomo) every Saturday at 17 hrs.

Confession is held before Mass on Wednesday, Friday, Saturday 10-12 hrs; and at the Church of the Hospital of St John of God, Via Borgo Ognissanti, every Sunday and Feast Day at 10 hrs.

Your representative can provide you with full details of other services in English.

Chapter Four

The great highlights

4.1 The historic setting

Founded by Julius Caesar in 59 BC as a military post to guard the Arno bridge, Florence remained a Roman city until the 5th century. The city's ideal position amid rich agricultural country helped Florence through the Dark Ages, and then to develop as a medieval commercial centre.

The economy boomed after Florence became a free commune in 1115. Based on wool trade, general commerce and industry, the city was ruled by an oligarchy of bankers and merchants. Despite constant feuds that lasted into the late 13th century, Florence continued to prosper. This was the age of Dante's romantic love for Beatrice, followed by his *Divine Comedy*.

During this period the Florentines began devoting their wealth to building the great monuments of today's sightseeing: the Cathedral, Santa Croce Church and the Palazzo Vecchio. The Ponte Vecchio in its present style came later, in 1345.

In 1348 the Black Death of bubonic plague halved the city population – an episode described in Boccaccio's *Decameron*. There followed a troubled period of misery and unrest and a revolt of the cloth-makers (the *Ciompi*) in 1378. But finally the city's growth picked up again, with wealthy patrons and the Church attracting the great artists and intellectuals of the day.

All this came to fruition with the **Medici dynasty** who ruled the city from 1434 to 1494; again from 1512 to 1527; and finally as hereditary rulers from 1530 to 1737. Their initial money and power came from trading and banking, with Cosimo as the first to exercise despotic rule from 1434 until his death in 1464.

His patronage of the arts laid the basis of the brilliant court culture of his grandson, Lorenzo the Magnificent. He surrounded himself with poets, painters and philosophers, and subsidized all the great artists of the Florentine Renaissance.

For an 18-year period, Florence was a Republic until Lorenzo's grandson – also named Lorenzo – regained power in 1512 and became Duke of Urbino. Later generations of Medici dukes ruled until the male line died out in 1737. The Medici art collections have survived almost intact – apart from some loss during the Napoleonic occupation – and form the basis of the Uffizi gallery, the Palatine Gallery, the Archaeological Museum and the Bargello Museum.

From 1865 until 1870, Florence was the capital of Italy, with the Pitti Palace used as the royal residence until the final reunification of Italy with Rome as capital.

During World War II, German forces destroyed all the Arno bridges except Ponte Vecchio. But the greater damage to Florentine art treasures came in 1966 when the historic centre was inundated by floods.

4.2 The Cathedral Square

The Piazza del Duomo is a very busy crossroads which has none of the tranquility that usually goes with a religious centre. But here are three superb buildings which have attracted visitors for centuries: the Baptistry, the Cathedral (Duomo) and the Bell Tower. Although different in style, each building is clad in contrasting slabs of black, white, green and pink marble to form a cheerful Florentine design.

Duomo – Cathedral Santa Maria del Fiore

The full grandeur of the Cathedral is best seen from a distance – from the hilltop of Piazzale Michelangelo across the river, for instance. The 13th-century assignment was to build a church which would rival anything produced by Pisa or Siena. Most of the building was completed by 1421. The architects were then faced with the baffling problem of crowning the Cathedral with a huge dome, of a size which was quite outside their technical experience.

The solution was worked out by Filippo Brunelleschi, who was a complete Renaissance man: painter, sculptor and goldsmith who also turned his hand to architecture. His cupola has delighted the world ever since. Among his other masterpieces in Florence are the Pazzi Chapel at Santa Croce, and the Pitti Palace.

The austere interior is a fine setting for the masterpieces it contains, including stained glass windows designed by Ghiberti and a clock decorated in 1443 with *Heads of Prophets* by Paolo Uccello. The *Pietà* by Michelangelo is now located in the Cathedral Museum (see below).

Baptistry

Facing the Cathedral's main door, the Baptistry is reckoned to be the oldest building in Florence, on the site of a 5th-century church where originally stood something Roman, details unknown. The existing structure dates from 11th century, and was completed 200 years later. For a century it served as Florence cathedral. Drawing the crowds for the past 600 years are three magnificent gilded bronze doors.

Oldest is the South Door, with 28 panels designed by Andrea Pisano in 1330, of which the top 20 panels represent the life of John the Baptist.

The contract for the North Door was awarded in 1402 to Lorenzo Ghiberti, following a competition in which five other leading artists including Brunelleschi also took part. The project occupied him and his collaborators – among them, Donatello and Uccello – for twenty years.

The Florentine guilds who financed the work were so pleased with the result that they commissioned Ghiberti to do the East Door as well. Ten framed squares depict Old Testament scenes, which took the Ghiberti team another thirty years to complete. Effectively, it set the seal on Florence as a major centre of sculpture, as well as painting. A century later, Michelangelo described that Baptistry door as "the gate of Paradise".

Giotto's Bell Tower, the Campanile

Standing alongside the Duomo, the Campanile designed by Giotto in 1334 is one of the great landmarks of Florence. Through its grace and harmony, the Bell Tower is considered to be the finest in Italy. It's well worth the climb of 414 steps for the splendid view of the city and of the Arno valley.
Open: 8.30-12.30 & 14.30-17.30 hrs. Entrance: 1500 lire.

Cathedral Museum
(Museo dell'Opera del Duomo)   Tel: 213229
Piazza del Duomo 9 – behind the apse of the Cathedral

The museum contains many works of art – sculpture, articles in gold, silver, embroidery etc – which were created to furnish the Cathedral, Campanile and Baptistry, but could not remain in place for security reasons. The *Pietà* is one of Michelangelo's last works, carved when he was 75 years' old, and planned for his own tomb.
Open: Summer – 9-20 hrs; Winter – 9-18 hrs; Sundays – 10-13 hrs.
Entrance: 4,000 lire. Free on Sunday.

4.3 Piazza della Signoria

Here is the vivid centre of Florentine life for the past 1,000 years – scene of civic quarrels and festivities, overlooked by the high tower of Palazzo della Signoria from which the Piazza takes its name. The Signoria was a democratic executive council set up in 1282. The Piazza still remains the centre of Florentine political and commercial life, with the Palace used as the Town Hall.

As you face towards the Palazzo della Signoria, a line of statues leads the eye towards the Uffizi, in the corner. Starting with the equestrian statue of Cosimo I in the centre of the Piazza, there's a

Neptune Fountain by the corner wall of the Palace; then a line-up of three statues, with a copy of Michelangelo's *David* in the middle. The original stood there from 1504 onwards, but was moved to the Accademia in 1873.

Next around the square is the open-plan Loggia dei Lanzi – a late 14th-century arcade built for public ceremonies, but now used as an open-air sculpture museum.

The steps also offer relief to exhausted sightseers.

NOTE: Try to avoid the crush in popular museums such as the Pitti Palace or the Uffizi. Weekdays, aim to enter around midday, when many visitors are ending their morning sightseeing. You'll then have a reasonably clear two hours before you go for a leisured lunch and siesta. Alternatively, queue up before the galleries open, and try to keep ahead of the tour groups.

4.4 The Uffizi Gallery
Loggiato degli Uffizi 6   Tel: 218341

The building itself was designed in 1560 as government offices (*uffici*) on the orders of Cosimo I. It stretches in two handsome wings from the Piazza della Signoria to the river. One wonders how many 20th-century civil service office blocks will give similar aesthetic pleasure, 400 years later.

The Uffizi Gallery is rated as the finest in Italy, and also the world's most important for Italian painting – particularly Florentine. The basic collection was amassed by the Medici, with additions by the dukes of Lorraine. Later, more paintings came from Tuscan churches and convents which felt unable to look after their treasures properly. Many other works have been purchased or donated.

Every age of Italian art is represented. Masterpieces are displayed room by room mainly in date order, and in sequence of styles, schools and regions. In this logical order, you can appreciate how one master influenced his pupils and successors; or you can jump direct to periods that interest you most. The best strategy is to see the Uffizi on a conducted tour, and then return at leisure direct to your favourite rooms. Many visitors concentrate on Rooms 7-15 on the second floor.

Room 2: 13th-century Tuscan School, including the two founders of Sienese and Florentine painting – Duccio di Buoninsegna, and Cimabue. See also the Giotto altarpiece of about 1310.

Room 3: 14th-century Sienese Gothic painting.

Room 4: Followers of Giotto – mainly Taddeo Gaddi and Bernardo Daddi.

Rooms 5 & 6: Giottesque and International Gothic styles, late 14th and early 15th century.

Room 7: Tuscan 15th century – the flowering of early Renaissance painting.

Room 8: Works by Filippo Lippi.

Room 9: The Pollaiuolo Brothers and early Botticelli.

Rooms 10-14: The Botticelli rooms: packed with the greatest works of the Medici collection.

Room 15: Leonardo da Vinci and Verrocchio, showing Leonardo's work as a teenager.

Room 16: The Map Room – frescoed maps by Buonsignori; and paintings by Hans Memling.

Room 18: The Tribune, designed in 1584 to house antique sculptures which particularly appealed to the Medici family. The widely-copied Medici Venus – itself a Roman copy of a Greek 4th-century BC model – aroused generations of Grand Tour visitors to an enthusiasm for art.

Room 19: Perugino.

Room 20: Dürer and other North European painters influenced by the Italian Renaissance.

Room 21: Bellini and Giorgione.

Room 22: Flemish and German painters, especially Holbein and his school.

Room 23: Correggio and other followers of Leonardo da Vinci.

Room 24: Miniatures by Italian and foreign artists, from 15th to 18th centuries.

Room 25: Raphael and Michelangelo, and their followers of the 'Mannerist' school.

Room 26: Andrea del Sarto, Raphael and the Mannerists.

Room 27: Pontormo.

Room 28: Titian – a rich selection, including the famous Venus of Urbino nude pin-up.

Room 29: Parmigianino and other late 16th-century painters.

Room 30: Parmigianino and Dosso Dossi.

Room 31: 16th century Venetians.

Room 34: Veronese and Tintoretto.

Room 35: Tintoretto and 16th-century Venetians – Baroccio.

Room 41: Rubens and Van Dyck.

Room 43: Caravaggio – *Bacchus*, *Medusa* and the *Sacrifice of Isaac*.

Room 44: Rembrandt, including a self-portrait.

Room 45: 18th-century Venetian, French and Spanish paintings.

Watch out for the *Wild Boar* in the exit hall.

Open: Tue-Sat 9-19 hrs; Sun 9-13 hrs.

Entrance: 10,000 lire

4.5 Ponte Vecchio

Crossing the River Arno at its narrowest point, the Ponte Vecchio – Old Bridge – was rebuilt in its present three-span form in 1345. The previous 10th-century bridge had been destroyed by flood; so the Ponte Vecchio was designed with durability in mind. It was solidly constructed to support two rows of shops, giving the bridge its present unique appearance of terraced houses with foundations in the river itself.

Originally those shops were fairly basic – tanners, butchers, blacksmiths, greengrocers. Then, in mid-16th century, the bridge moved up-market when a second-floor corridor was built to link the Palazzo Vecchio with the new grand-ducal Pitti Palace. In the cause of civic dignity, Ferdinand I in 1593 ordered out the 'vile trades', to be replaced by fifty goldsmiths and jewellers at double the rent. The shops were later extended over the river, with the back-developments supported by wooden beams.

Four centuries later, Ponte Vecchio is still a centre for the gold and jewellery trade, and more recently a nighttime venue for street musicians. Halfway across the bridge is a bronze bust of Benvenuto Cellini, greatest of the goldsmiths.

4.6 Pitti Palace & the Palatine Gallery

Originally built by the Pitti family in 15th century to be one-up on their Medici rivals across the river, the Pitti Palace was finally acquired by the Medici dynasty in 1549, when the Pittis fell on hard times.

Many extensions were made over the following centuries, to make a fitting Medici ducal residence. Finally the Pitti Palace became a royal residence of the Savoia family (1865-71). Today the Pitti Palace houses several museums: the Palatine Gallery, the Silver Museum and the Modern Art Gallery.

In the **Palatine Gallery**, priceless paintings hang against a sumptuous gilt, stuccoed and frescoed decor, all left as hung according to the personal taste of the last Medici and later Grand Dukes, when it was all part of their private collection. There was no attempt at chronological order, as in the Uffizi. The gallery includes works by Botticelli, Raphael, Titian, Rubens, Velasquez and Murillo.

The Silver Museum may also be visited on Wednesday, Friday and Saturday using the same ticket. It contains a rich collection of greatly-varied pieces made of gold, silver, ivory and amber. Here's the luxury craftsmanship which a family of unlimited wealth could buy during the 16th and 17th centuries.

Open: Tue-Sat 9-14 hrs; Sun 9-13 hrs
Entrance: 6,000 lire   Tel: 210323

Gallery of Modern Art, Piazza dei Pitti
On the second floor of the Pitti Palace, the modern art collection is housed in some 30 rooms. Discover the exciting Macchiaioli ('blotch painters'), Tuscany's own Impressionist movement of the 1860's – see rooms 23-26.

Open: Tue-Sat 9-14 hrs; Sun 9-13 hrs.
Entrance: 8,000 lire.   Tel: 287096

Chapter Five

The Church as art patron

5.1 Santa Maria Novella Cloisters

Close to Central Station   Tel: 282187

The 'new' church dates from 1278, when Dominican monks replaced an earlier 10th century church. The stunning facade is green and white marble in Renaissance style, designed by Leon Battista Alberti.

The Cloisters give access to the Spanish Chapel, decorated around 1366 by Andrea da Firenze and his assistants as a tribute to the Dominican Order.

Open: Mon-Sat 9-19 hrs (closed Friday); Sun 8-13 hrs. Entrance: 3,000 lire (free on Sunday).

5.2 Santa Croce

Founded in 1294, and known as Italy's Westminster Abbey, the Gothic basilica of Santa Croce contains tombs and monuments to many of the great men of Florence: Dante, Michelangelo, Machiavelli, Galileo and Rossini. The largest and most famous Franciscan church in Italy, Santa Croce has rich decorations including Giotto's frescoes which had great influence on Florentine painters.

Cloisters lead to Brunelleschi's Pazzi Chapel and the Santa Croce Museum.

Santa Croce Museum (Museo Cimabue)

Includes works from artists such as Donatello, Cimabue, Veneziano, de Banco and Gaddi.

Open: Winter 10.00-12.30 & 15-17 hrs. (Closed Wed). Summer 10.00-12.30 & 14.30-18.30 hrs. Entrance: 3,000 lire.   Tel: 244619

Piazza Santa Croce

This lively square, with a statue of Dante wrapped in a toga, has a long history as a craft centre. In the 14th century it was the heart of the dyeing and tanning trades, closely linked with Florentine prosperity from wool and leather manufacture. Leather and other crafts still flourish around the Piazza, greatly supported by tourist business.

5.3 The Medici Chapels

Piazza di Madonna degli Aldobrandini, behind the church of S. Lorenzo

The New Sacristy was designed by Michelangelo in 1524. Most of the Medici Grand Dukes, and members of their families, are buried here, glorified in masterpieces of sculpture.

Open: Tue-Sat 9-14 hrs; Sun 9-13 hrs.
Entrance: 8,000 lire.   Tel: 213206

5.4 San Marco Museum

This Dominican monastery, rebuilt and decorated in 15th century, was focal point of Florentine culture throughout the Renaissance. In the 1490's, San Marco was the turbulent centre of religious fervour inspired by Savonarola, the demagogue Prior of San Marco.

Since 1869 this building has served like a one-man exhibition centre for the works of Fra Angelico and his pupils: panel paintings from other churches and galleries, his *Annunciation*, and particularly the frescoes in 44 dormitory cells, painted by the friar and his assistants. Among the other works are paintings by Fra Bartolomeo.

Open: Tue-Sat 9-14 hrs; Sun 9-13 hrs.
Entrance: 6,000 lire.   Tel: 210741

5.5 Churches

Church of Santo Spirito, Piazza Santo Spirito

Designed by Filippo Brunelleschi, this typical 15th-century Renaissance church is rich in art treasures – though many of the original works from the 39 semi-circular chapels have been removed to museums.

Orsanmichele in Via dei Calzaiuoli was originally a grain market, converted into a church from 1380, with upper floors used for emergency grain stores.

In early 15th century, 21 of the Florentine guilds each supplied a statue of their patron saint, with several of the commissions going to Ghiberti and to Donatello. Open: 7-12 & 14-19 hrs.

All Saints' Church (Church of Ognissanti)
Founded in mid-13th century, the church was converted to Baroque style in 17th century. This church was the burial place of the family of Amerigo Vespucci, the Florentine explorer who gave his name to America. A fresco painted about 1470 – *Madonna of Mercy Sheltering the Vespucci Family* – includes a reputed portrait of Amerigo as a lad. A family tombstone is left of the altar. The explorer was born 1454 in the family home, Palazzo Vespucci, located close by in Borgo Ognissanti.

Church of the Carmine
(Santa Maria del Carmine), Piazza del Carmine
Worth visiting to see frescoes in the Brancacci Chapel, mostly painted around 1425-1428 by a young genius named Masaccio. Although only 27 when he died, Masaccio's work had enormous influence on the greatest of Renaissance painters – Michelangelo included – who closely studied his pioneer techniques of depicting space and perspective. The most famous of the seven frescoes by Masaccio is *Payment of the Tribute by Christ*.

Santa Trinità, Piazza Santa Trinità
11th century church erected by the Vallombrosan Monks.

San Miniato Al Monte, Monte alle Croci
One of the most beautiful Romanesque churches in Italy, San Miniato was built in 11th century, and decorated in Florentine style with a green and white marble facade. Mosaics were added in 13th century and restored in the 19th. From its hilltop site, the visitor has a splendid view over Florence.

Chapter Six

The classic viewpoints

Central Florence with its narrow streets and high buildings can make you yearn for air. Here are three suggestions for a wider view.

Boboli Gardens, Pitti Palace
An Italian court garden of cypress and hedge-lined alleys, with unusual statuary, grottoes and fountains. Handy place for a picnic after visiting the Pitti Palace museums and the Palatine Gallery!
Open daily at 9 a.m., closing near sunset.

Fiesole
Take a 30-minute drive north of Florence by no. 7 bus. The ride is delightful, winding up a hill bordered with beautiful gardens and villas and finally running into the central square.

Fiesole was an Etruscan settlement, then Roman. A music and film festival is held July-August in the 1st-century BC Roman theatre, seating 3000.

Piazzale Michelangelo
Take bus no. 13 to this Piazza on a hillside 300 feet above the Arno, offering a classic view over the whole of Florence and out to the hills of Tuscany. Left to right are the church tower of Santa Maria Novella, the bell-tower of Palazzo Vecchio, the Cathedral with its splendid cupola and adjoining Campanile, the Basilica of Santa Croce and the green dome of the Synagogue.

In the centre of the square is a copy of Michelangelo's *David*, and of his statues symbolising *Day, Night, Dawn* and *Dusk*.

Chapter Seven

Palaces, museums and galleries

7.1 Embarrassment of riches

Florence has over twenty art museums and still more historic palaces and mansions. It's impossible to see *everything* in a three-night stay. Here's a brief listing of some more treasures to visit if time permits.

Note that entrance fees, opening times and closing days of Museums and Galleries are all liable to change. So be prepared. Most museums close one day a week, usually either Monday or Tuesday. Staff problems or renovations can close entire museum sections, sometimes for months. Before making a special journey, check on opening hours.

On the principal public holidays, virtually all shops, museums and galleries are closed. The compensation is that Florence is then a one-day paradise for pedestrians.

7.2 More palaces

Palazzo Vecchio (Palazzo della Signoria)

Piazza Signoria   Tel: 21644

Ranking as the finest medieval building in Italy, the Palazzo della Signoria was founded in 1299 and was the early seat of government. This building, topped by a superb watch tower, witnessed many violent events in the city's history. As a centre of intrigue, the *cancelleria* was Machiavelli's office in the early years of the 16th century.

In 1540, the Medici ruler Cosimo I had the fortress-like Palazzo converted into his personal residence, suitably decorated with frescoes which paid fulsome tribute to himself and his ancestors. Afterwards, Cosimo moved to the Pitti Palace, and this building became known as the Old Palace – Palazzo Vecchio. It is now used as City Hall.

With all that history in mind, the Palazzo Vecchio is worth a visit: particularly to see the great hall built in 1496, and the works of art on the 2nd floor.

Open: Mon-Fri 9-19 hrs; Sun 8-13 hrs. Closed Sat. Entrance: 8,000 lire.

Palazzo Medici-Riccardi, Via Cavour 1

The palace was built 1444-1464 by the Medici family, who used it as their residence until they moved to the Palazzo Vecchio.

This style of palace architecture became the standard for other wealthy families during the height of Florentine prosperity.

Visit the tiny family chapel to see Benozzo Gozzoli's fresco *Procession of the Magi*. Painted in 1459, the entire family is right there, together with anyone else who counted in Florence at that time!

Open: Mon-Sat 9-12.30 & 15-17 hrs. Closed Wed. Sunday 9-12 hrs. Entrance: 2,000 lire.

Casa di Dante, Via S. Margherita 1

Here are the reconstructed houses which belonged to the Alighieri family. Dante Alighieri, greatest of Italian poets, was born here in 1265. A small museum displays reproductions of Botticelli's illustrations for Dante's work, and portraits of the poet. Open: 9.30-12.30 & 15.30-18.30; Sunday 9.30-12.30 hrs. Closed Wednesday.   Tel: 283343

7.3 More museums and galleries
The Academy Gallery

The Galleria dell'Accademia at Via Ricasoli 60 is best known for its Michelangelo sculptures, including the original of *David* which stood in Piazza della Signoria until removed in 1873 as protection from the weather.

This statue of Carrara marble permanently set Michelangelo's fame as one of the world's greatest sculptors. His four powerful but unfinished *Slaves* were intended for a papal mausoleum in Rome.

The Academy Gallery was created in 1784, and is devoted mainly to Florentine paintings of 13th to 16th centuries, with more recent additions of 18th and 19th century academic works.
Open: Tue-Sat 9-14 hrs; Sun 9-13 hrs.
Entrance: 10,000 lire.   Tel: 214375

National Sculpture Museum – Il Bargello,

Via del Proconsolo   Tel: 210801
Built as a town hall in 1255, the palace later became the residence of the Captain of Justice (Bargello). As police headquarters, part of the building was used for torture and executions. Since 1859 the Bargello has served as the National Sculpture Museum, with medieval and Renaissance masterpieces, and ceramics, coins, arms and armour.
Open: Tue-Sat 9-14; Sun 9-13 hrs.
Entrance: 6,000 lire.

Galleria dello Spedale degli Innocenti

Gallery of the Hospital of the Innocents
Piazza SS. Annunziata 12
An early 15th-century home for foundlings, now houses pictures, sculptures, miniatures and furniture dating from the 14th to 18th centuries.
Open: Winter 9-13 hrs (closed Wednesday).
Summer (June-Oct) 9-19 hrs. Entrance 3,000 lire.

Anthropology Museum

Via del Proconsolo 12   Tel: 296449
A worldwide collection of ethnic interest.
Open: Thu-Sat and first & third Sunday of the month 9-13 hrs. Closed July-September.

Archaeological Museum, Via della Colonna 38

In the 17th-century Palazzo della Crocetta, the museum houses an outstanding collection of Egyptian, Etruscan and Greco-Roman finds.
Open: Tue-Sat 9-14 hrs; Sun 9-13 hrs.
Entrance: 6,000 lire   Tel: 215270

Bardini Museum & Corsi Gallery

Piazza de' Mozzi   Tel: 296749

Donated in 1923 by Stefano Bardini, a wealthy art dealer – a 20-room collection of wood, plaster and terra-cotta sculptures from Etruscan times to medieval; also 17th-century Florentine tapestries.
Open: Mon-Sat 9-14 hrs (closed Wed). Sun 8-13 hrs. Closed on some holidays, please check.
Entrance: 5,000 lire.

Florence As it Used to Be
(Museo di Firenze com'era)

Via dell'Oriuolo 24   Tel: 217305

An exhibition of paintings, prints and photographs relating to the city's physical history. This building was formerly a monastery.
Open: Mon-Sat 9-14 hrs (closed Thur); Sun 8-13 hrs. Entrance: 3,000 lire.

History of Science Museum, Piazza dei Giudici

From an alchemist's laboratory to the telescope with which Galileo discovered the four 'Medici satellites' of Jupiter.
Open: 9.30-13 hrs & 14-17 hrs. Closed Tue, Thu, Saturday a.m., Sunday and public holidays.
Entrance: 5,000 lire.   Tel: 293493

Michelangelo Museum – Casa Buonarrotti

Via Ghibellina 70   Tel: 241752

Michelangelo bought the house for his nephew, Leonardo di Buonarotti, but never lived in it himself. Leonardo's son, Michelangelo the Younger, decorated the house and turned it into a memorial to the great artist.
Open: Mon-Sat 9.30-13.30 hrs (closed Tue); Sun 9-12.30 hrs. Entrance: 5,000 lire.

Chapter Eight

Go shopping

8.1 Stylish boutiques

Florence is one of Europe's great shopping cities. Jewellery stores are grouped on, and around, Ponte Vecchio. And there are world-famed fashion houses, shoe and knitwear stores, in the central shopping streets. In fact, Florentine fashion is as highly renowned as Parisian. The city is crammed with hundreds of fascinating little boutiques. Whether you wish to spoil yourself or not, window shopping in Florence is a delight!

Many craft workshops are centred around the Piazza Santa Croce, where you can stop by to watch the skilled hand production of leather, silver and mosaic in studios that follow centuries'-old traditions.

Opening hours follow the normal Italian pattern: Summer: 9-13 & 16-20 hrs. Winter: 9-13 & 15.30-19.30 hrs.

From 15 June-15 September, shops close on Saturday afternoon; during the rest of the year, on Monday morning. Food shops close on Wednesday afternoons.

8.2 What to buy

Jewellery – Gold & silver can be surprisingly cheap in Florence, though the more creative the item, the more expensive it is. Look for pill-boxes, napkin rings, photo frames and candlesticks.

Glassware – Attractive, functional glassware, often very reasonably priced, is available from Empoli or Pisa.

Leather – This is exquisite! Best buys are gloves, belts, purses, wallets and boxes of all shapes and sizes. It is usually possible to have your initials stamped in gold leaf on any purchase.

Antiques – These abound, and are invariably pricey. Bric-a-brac is practically non-existent.

8.3 Shopping areas

Fashion Boutiques – Via de'Tornabuoni, Via de'Calzaìuouli (smart and expensive).

Leather – San Lorenzo, Santa Croce (Don't miss the leather school tucked away behind Santa Croce's sacristy in former Franciscan monks' cells).

Gold & Silver – Ponte Vecchio.

Inlays & Mosaics – Lungarno Torrigiani, Via Guicciardini, Piazza Santa Croce.

Antiques – Borgo Ognissanti, San Jacopo, Via della Vigna Nuova, Via della Spada, Piazza del Duomo.

Other areas worth visiting:
Via Strozzi; Via Porta Rossa; Via Roma; Via del Parione; Via dei Pecori; Piazza della Repubblica.

Shops – These are inevitably too numerous to list, but for quality goods at reasonable prices try:

Leather at 'Fibbi', Corsa dei Tintori 19/12. Open 9-19 hrs daily. Closed on Sundays Dec-Feb.

Gold & Silver, 18 KT, Via S. Giuseppe 32r, Santa Croce. All items are sold by weight and carry 18 carat hallmark.

Markets

San Lorenzo, Piazza San Lorenzo
Everything from mouth-watering fresh food to leather handbags! Prices are reasonable, and some stalls accept credit cards and traveller's cheques.

Mercato Nuovo (Flea Market)
A score of stalls offering straw bags, sun hats, trinkets, jewellery, etc.

Piazza dei Ciompi (Flea Market)
Open daily in full season. Many interesting bits and pieces.

Mercato Cascine
Located in Cascine Park. Sells everything. Held on Tuesday mornings.

8.4 Clothing Sizes

There is no exact science about conversions between British, North American and Italian clothing sizes. The following figures offer some rough guidance as a prelude to trying on garments before purchase.

Women's dresses and suits

British	32	34	36	38	40	42
or British	6	8	10	12	14	16
USA	4	6	8	10	12	14
Italian	38	40	42	44	46	48

Men's suits and coats

UK & USA	36	38	40	42	44	46
Italian	46	48	50	52	54	56

Men's Shirts

UK & USA	14½	15	15½	16	16½	17
Italian	37	38	39	40	42	43

Women's Shoes

UK	2	3	4	5	6	7	8
USA	3	4	5	6	7	8	9
Italian	34	36	37	38	39	40	41

Men's Shoes

UK	5	6	7	8	9	10	11
USA	6	7	8	9	10	11	12
Italian	38	39	41	42	43	44	46

Chapter Nine

Take a trip

9.1 Visit Pisa

Although Florence is so packed with city-centre interest, try to make time to see something of the Tuscan countryside. Thanks to excellent bus and rail connections, trips to all parts of Tuscany are easily arranged. If you don't want to rent a car, there is good choice of coach excursions.

Only 50 miles away is Pisa, where everything focusses on the 'Miracle Square': the Romanesque Cathedral, the Baptistry and of course the Leaning Tower. This unique group of buildings has survived since the 12th century – witness to the former power and prosperity of the ancient Maritime Republic which once rivalled Venice and Genoa.

With its shallow natural harbour at the mouth of the River Arno, Pisa's bad luck was that the sea retreated from 13th century onwards. Pisa progressively declined as the harbour silted up.

But Pisa's reputation as a university town has remained intact, particularly strong in science ever since the stirring times when Galileo lectured here. In the Cathedral hangs the swinging bronze lamp which first set Galileo's mind working in 1581 on the mathematics of pendulum movement. Ten years later, he used the Leaning Tower for his famous demonstration that objects with different weights fall with identical velocity.

Scientific matters apart, the Cathedral is forested with Corinthian columns. An early 14th-century pulpit by Giovanni Pisano is a masterpiece of sculpture, with panels that depict New Testament scenes. Look also at the 16th-century bronze doors.

Leaning Tower

Despite tilting 15 feet out of plumb, the Leaning Tower is in no immediate danger. However, the authorities no longer permit visitors to climb 294 steps up the inner spiral staircase for a pigeon's-eye view over the cathedral roof.

Cemeteries don't usually rate high on sightseeing itineraries, but it's worth visiting the Camposanto behind the cathedral. Although badly war-damaged in 1944, the cemetery is famed for its frescoes and sculptures.

9.2 Siena

Due south of Florence is the beautifully-preserved medieval town of Siena, which demands a full day to appreciate the rolling Chianti hills and vineyards, preferably with time for San Gimignano en route.

Inside the original city walls of Siena is medieval perfection, with a street plan virtually unchanged from 13th century. Buildings are the colour of burnt sienna from bricks made of local red clay. Motor traffic is banned from the centre – a maze of winding streets that finally empty into the principal Piazza del Campo.

The Campo, fan-shaped like a shell, offers a truly theatrical setting for the traditional *Palio* horse race, bareback and in medieval costume. The contest has been an integral part of the Siena calendar for centuries, based on intense rivaly between the seventeen *contrada* or wards into which the city has been divided since medieval times. The race is held on July 2, with a repeat performance on August 16. Tickets are very expensive and difficult to obtain, but you can often see rehearsals on the previous days.

However, if you cannot make those dates, Siena is still a fantastic city to explore. You could spend your time entirely in the Campo, enjoying what could easily rate as Italy's most beautiful square.

Among the historic buildings to visit are the Cathedral, the Town Hall, and the rival Dominican and Franciscan Churches of San Domenico and San Francesco.

San Gimignano

Well-organised coach tours to Siena often include a visit to San Gimignano – another superb medieval survival, from which happily all 20th-century traffic is excluded. There are charming old streets and squares and towers, little changed from the year 1300 when the poet Dante came here on a diplomatic mission from Florence.

Seven hundred years ago, most Italian hilltop fortified cities were built in this style, ringed with walls and defensive turrets. Formerly San Gimignano was equipped with 70 towers, of which 13 still dominate the skyline, overlooking the surrounding countryside of vineyards and olive groves. Today's traveller can enjoy the same beautiful landscape that was portrayed by medieval and Renaissance artists. The 15th-century fresco painter Benozzo Gozzoli was born here. Though he worked mainly in Florence and Pisa, he spent four years on the frescoes in the church of San Agostino.

Don't miss San Gimignano! If you have time for only one day's excursion outside of Florence, pick this one.

9.3 Two-centre breaks

A popular idea is to split a week on a two-centre citybreak that links Florence with Rome or Venice. Florence is neatly located halfway between those two cities, with excellent train links in each direction. Reckon around 3½ hours either way, north or south.

The connecting rail journey itself is a delight, with good scenery to watch. Travel in Italian style, buying a bottle of wine and some paper cups to keep thirst at bay. En route between Florence and Venice, be alert for a halt at Bologna station. There, clued-up travellers lean out the window and buy piping-hot cartons of green lasagne from mobile trolleys that come dashing along. Delicious!

Chapter Ten

Learn Italian

Don't worry if you cannot speak Italian. In the main hotels, restaurants, bars and shops, service staff have at least a smattering of most West European languages. If not, there's always someone handy who can translate.

However, there's pleasure in being able to use and recognise even just a few words. Pronunciation is quite straightforward, reasonably phonetic.

The following letters are pronounced as in English: *b, d, f, l, m, n, t, v.*

For the vowels, pronounce:

a as in English p*a*st;

e has two sounds – as in p*e*st or p*a*ste;

i as in pr*ie*st;

o has two sounds – as in p*o*st or p*o*t;

u as in b*oo*st.

The tricky consonants are:

c as in *ch*ase or *ch*eese before *e* and *i*;

  as in *c*ast, *c*ost or *c*oot before *a, o* or *u.*

g as in *g*ender or *g*enes before *e* and *i*;

  as in *g*arnish, *g*olf or *g*oose before *a, o* or *u.*

z has two sounds – as in mai*ds* or as in ba*ts.*

Some consonants are twinned for special effects:

ch before *e* or *i* becomes hard like a *k.*

gh before *e* or *i* becomes hard as in *gh*etto.

gl before *i* becomes liquid as in bi*lli*ards.

gn before all vowels is pronounced as in o*ni*on.

qu as in *qu*ality.

The Italian language does not use *k, w, x* or *y.*

For the beginner in Italian, we give a starter kit of a few words to show you're trying.

Greetings

Good morning	Buon giorno
Good afternoon	Buon pomeriggio
Good evening	Buona sera
How are you?	Come sta?
Very well, thank you	Benissimo, grazie
Goodbye	Arrivederci!
Good night	Buona notte

The essentials

Yes	Sì
No	No
Please	Per favore
Thank you	Grazie
Don't mention it	Prego
Excuse me! (on bus, etc)	Permesso!
Do you speak English?	Parla inglese?
I don't understand	Non capisco
At what time?	A che ora?

Money

Where is the bank?	Dov'è la banca?
Currency exchange	Cambio
I want to change $50.	Desidero cambiare cinquanta dollari.
How much is this?	Quanto costa questo?
Something cheaper	Qualcosa più a buon mercato
Too expensive!	Troppo caro!

Shopping

Chemist	la farmacia
Doctor	il medico; dottore
Hairdresser	parrucchiere
Post office	ufficio postale
Supermarket	supermercato
Tobacconist	la tabaccheria
I want to buy...	Voglio comprare...
a city map	una carta della città
some cigarettes	delle sigarette
some stamps	dei francobolli
postcards	cartoline postali
English newspapers	giornali inglesi

Sightseeing

Where is the …?	Dov'è … ?
bridge	il ponte
cathedral	la cattedrale
church	la chiesa
museum	il museo
opera house	l'Opera
palace	il palazzo
square	la piazza
station	la stazione
street	la strada
theatre	il teatro
Turn left, right	volti a sinistra, destra
Go straight ahead	vada diritto
Is it open on Sundays?	È aperto la domenica?
When was it built?	Quando fu costuito?

Signs

Aperto	open
Caldo	hot
Chiuso	closed
Donne	ladies
Elevatore	lift/elevator
Entrata	entrance
Freddo	cold
Gabinetto	toilet
Libero	free, vacant
Occupato	occupied
Pericolo	danger
Signori	gents
Silenzio	silence
Spingere	push
Tirare	pull
Uomini	gents
Uscita	exit
Vietato fumare	no smoking
Vietato l'ingresso	no entrance

Days of the week

Monday to Sunday – Lunedì, martedì, mercoledì, gioverdì, venerdì, sabato, domenica.

Today	oggi
Tomorrow	domani
Yesterday	ieri

Months

January to December – gennaio, febbraio, marzo, aprile, maggio, giugno, luglio, agosto, settembre, ottobre, novembre, dicembre.

Numbers

0	zero
1-10	uno, due, tre, quattro, cinque, sei, sette, otto,nove, dieci
11-19	undici, dodici, tredici, quattordici, quindici, sedici, diciasette, diciotto, diciannove
20-29	venti, ventuno, ventidue, ventitre etc.
30-39	trenta, trentuno, trentadue etc.
40-90	quaranta, cinquanta, sessanta, settanta, ottanta, novanta

100	cento	101	centouno
143	centoquarantatre	200	duecento
1000	mille	2000	duemila
1,000,000	un milione		

First, second, third   primo, secondo, terzo

The menu

Please see the next chapter for a food and drink vocabulary.

Chapter Eleven

Eating and drinking

11.1 Eating out in Florence

Florence can be enjoyed sitting down. The locals spend much of their leisure at pavement cafés, gossiping and watching the world go by. Favourite drinks are tiny, extra-strong cups of Espresso coffee, or apéritifs like Campari soda.

There is great choice of café locations: in 16th-century piazzas, echoing with children at play; in side-streets, friendly as a village pub; at busy cross-roads, providing ringside seats for the cut-and-thrust blood sport of Italian driving.

Food? Just like everywhere else in Italy, there is good eating almost anywhere you go. Restaurants offer a Menu Turistico at fixed all-inclusive prices, and there are fast-food establishments of every type. But Florence has colourful restaurants by the dozen, and it's worth devoting part of your city break to the enjoyment of good food in surroundings that are loaded with atmosphere.

Living to eat – not eating to live – is part of the Tuscan way of life. Florentines themselves prefer simple 'country' fare, and are somewhat unadventurous about exotic dishes from other countries. But there's enough variety in Italian cuisine – based on superbly fresh local fruit and vegetables – that you have no need to look further afield to eat well.

Part of the pleasure of a city break in Florence is to explore local and other regional dishes, and the Tuscany wines. It's much more fun than eating standard 'international' hotel menus. Don't worry if you cannot speak Italian - just wave and point. But most waiters have basic English.

Restaurant choice

Italy features three main kinds of restaurant – *osteria*, *trattoria* and *ristorante*, in ascending order of quality and price, though nowadays the distinction is blurring.

If you cannot manage a full meal at lunch-time, there are plenty of chances for snacks. Many bars have a selection of sandwiches called *tramezzini* which have very appetising fillings.

There's another type of restaurant/café called *tavola calda*, where you can get simple hot dishes at reasonable price. They are many of them in central Florence. Customers eat standing up – dishes of spaghetti, ravioli or whatever the dish of the day happens to be. It's very handy for a quick lunch, if you don't want a full sit-down meal spread over a couple of hours.

At a pizzeria, you can fill up with a bowl of thick minestrone and a huge pizza that overlaps a dinner plate.

For picnic eating, there is good, cheap fruit - oranges, cherries, melons, peaches, apricots, grapes, fresh figs, according to season. Excellent cheeses, cooked meats and salads help keep outgoings low.

Learn the Italian word *etto*, which means hectogramme or 100 grammes. For quick guidance, reckon it's a quarter-pound or four ounces. Fish or steak dishes are frequently priced per *etto*, not per portion. Know the system, and save yourself a nasty shock when the bill comes.

Quick snacks

There is something very typically Italian about the snack bars dominated by a massive Espresso machine, gleaming and polished and steaming. On the shelves behind are bottles of every conceivable spirit and liqueur known to European man. These establishments are also useful as a stopping-point for a quick sandwich.

In the mornings from 7 to 11 a.m. you'll find Italians having their breakfasts of cappuccinos and cornettos (croissants). However, if you feel in need of a brandy, you will not be on your own!

Bar codes

If you take a drink at the bar, you must normally pay first at the cash desk (cassa). Take the receipt to the bar, put a 100- or 200-lire coin on top of it (watch the Romans here), and tell the barman what you want. The tip ensures rapid service. Standing at the bar is always much cheaper than having drinks and sandwiches served to a table. You're not supposed to buck the system by ordering at the bar, and then sitting down.

In restaurants, a standard 'menu turistico' comprises a flat-rate 3-course menu, usually with a drink such as beer or quarter-litre of wine, service and tax. The price may be reasonable enough, but don't expect any gastronomic delights.

All restaurants charge 'coperto', which is a cover charge. Then there is a service charge which can add 10-20% on the total bill. Tipping is not necessary on top, unless for exceptional service. VAT is added. Keep the bill, as tax inspectors are making valiant attempts to keep tabs on the catering trade. Within 60 metres of a restaurant, inspectors can ask you to produce your receipt: otherwise, a hefty fine. However, for the foreign tourist, it's all rather theoretical.

11.2 Plenty of Pasta

In Italy you can eat pasta twice a day during a one-week citybreak, and come nowhere near repeating yourself. The variations on the pasta theme are enormous. It comes mainly in two colours: the usual cream colour; and green, made by working spinach into the paste. It's also made in a huge variety of shapes. Lifetime students of pasta break down mamma's favourite food into five main categories:

- Rope or string, e.g. Spaghetti
- Ribbon, e.g. Tagliatelle
- Tubes, e.g. Penne
- Envelopes, e.g. Ravioli
- Fancy shapes like shells or wheels, such as Conchiglie, Tortellini.

Pasta short-list

Agnolotti/ Anolini	Small stuffed envelopes, like ravioli
Cannelloni	Large tubes, stuffed with various meat, and baked in cheese and tomato sauce
Cappellitti	Twists of pasta, usually stuffed and served in a light sauce. The Roman version of tortellini.
Conchiglie	Shell-shaped pasta
Farfalloni	Pasta in the shape of a butterfly
Fettuccine	Thin ribbon pasta made with egg. The Roman name for tagliatelle.
Fusilli	Skeins of ribbon pasta
Lasagne	Ribbon pasta, usually baked after boiling
Lasagne verdi	Green lasagne
Penne	Small tubes
Pastina	Small, fine pasta in a variety of shapes for soup
Ravioli	Small envelopes, stuffed with a meat, vegetable or cheese filling
Rigatoni	Large grooved tubes
Spaghetti	Need more be said? But spaghetti can still be sub-divided into capellini, fusilli, spaghettini, spirale and vermicelli.
Tagliatelle	Ribbon pasta about a quarter or an inch wide
Tortellini	Little twists of pasta with a rich stuffing and delicate sauces
Tortelloni	Large coils of stuffed pasta

11.3 Guide to the menu

Zuppe e Antipasti	*Soups and Starters*
Gamberetti	Shrimps
Granchio	Crabs
Melone con fichi	Melon with figs
Melone con prosciutto	Melon with ham
Misto or frutti di mare	Mixed seafood
Panada	Broth
Zuppa di pesce	Fish soup
Zuppa di fagioli	Bean soup

Risotti e Pasta	*Rice and Pasta dishes*
Asparagi	Risotto with asparagus
Nere de seppie	Risotto with cuttlefish in its ink
Primavera	Risotto with diced fresh vegetables
Bigoli	Dark coloured pasta
Pasta e fagioli	Pasta with white bean soup
Risi e Anguilla	Rice and eel
Risi e bisi	Rice and peas

Pesce e Crostacei	*Fish and shellfish*
Anguilla	Eel
Aringa	Herring
Baccala	Cod
Branzino	Sea bass
Calamari	Squid
Cozze	Mussels
Frutta di mare	Seafood
Gamberelli	Prawns
Granchi	Shrimps
Nasello	Haddock
Ostriche	Oysters
Pesce spada	Swordfish
Salmone	Salmon
Sgombro	Mackerel
Sogliola	Plaice
Sogliola Finta	Sole
Tonno	Tuna
Triglia	Red Mullet
Trota	Trout

Carne	*Meat*
Agnello	Lamb
Anatra/anitra	Duck
Bistecca	Steak
Bistecca de Filetto	Fillet steak
Braciola	Cutlet, chop
Bue	Beef
Coniglio	Rabbit
Coscia	Leg
Cotoletta/Costata	Cutlet/chop
Fagiona	Pheasant
Faraona	Pheasant

Fegato	Liver
Maiale	Pork
Manzo	Beef
Montone	Mutton
Pollo	Chicken
Prosciutto	Ham
Ragout	Stew
Rognoni	Kidneys
Rosbif	Roast beef
Salsicce	Sausage
Salsicce alla Griglia	Grilled sausage
Selvaggina	Venison
Tacchino	Turkey
Tournedo	Rump steak
Vitello	Veal

Verdura	*Vegetables*
Aglio	Garlic
Barbabietola/Bietola	Beetroot
Broccoli	Broccoli
Carciofi	Artichokes
Carotte	Carrots
Cavolfiore	Cauliflower
Cetriolo	Cucumber
Cipolle	Onions
Fagioli	Beans
Funghi	Mushrooms
Insalata	Salad
Lattuga	Lettuce
Melanzana	Aubergines
Patate	Potatoes
Peperoni	Peppers
Piselli	Peas
Pomodoro	Tomato
Spinaci	Spinach

Dolci	*Desserts*
Bussolai	Traditional biscuits from Burano
Gelato	Ice cream
Tirami su	Rich dessert soaked in coffee and liqueur, and covered in cream
Zuppa inglese	Trifle

| Zabaglione | Dessert made with egg yolks and Marsala |

Frutta	*Fruit*
Albicocca	Apricot
Ananas	Pineapple
Anguria	Water melon
Arancia	Orange
Cillege	Cherries
Fragole	Strawberries
Frutta fresca	Fresh fruit
Lamponi	Raspberries
Mela	Apple
Pera	Pear
Pesca	Peach
Pompelino	Grapefruit
Prugna	Plum

Bibite	*Drinks*
Acqua Minerale	Mineral water
Birra	Beer
Caffè	Black coffee
Cappucino	White coffee
Latte	Milk
Tè	Tea
Vino – rosso, bianco	Wine – red, white
dolce, secco, spumante	– sweet, dry, sparkling

Miscellaneous

Burro	Butter
Formaggio	Cheese
Frittata	Omelette
Gnocchi	Dumplings
Minestra	Soup
Pane	Bread
Salsa	Sauce
Uova	Eggs

Cooking terms

Arrosto	Roast
Crudo	Cured
Cotto	Cooked
Stufato	Stew

11.4 Typical Tuscan specialities
Antipasto
Finocchiona - A kind of salami flavoured with fennel seeds
Crostini – Open chopped liver sandwiches

First Course
Ribollita – A thick bread and vegetable soup
Cacciucco alla Livornnese – Fish stew with a very hot sauce
Pappardelle alla Lepre – Pasta with hare sauce
Tortino di Carciofi – Baked artichoke pie
Baccala alla Livornese – Salt cod cooked in tomatoes, black olives and black pepper

Main Course
Bistecca alla Fiorentina – A tasty steak which weighs about a kilo, and is enough for 2 people. Make sure to be very hungry, before ordering!
Arista – Herb flavoured roast pork
Stracotto – Beef lengthily cooked in red wine
Trippa – Tripe cooked in tomatoes and onions

Side Dishes
Fagioli al fiasco – Beans cooked in a glass flask
Fagioli all'Uccelletto - Haricot beans cooked with tomatoes, sage and garlic
Frittura mista – Batter fried zucchini (courgettes), artichokes and other seasonal vegetables

Desserts
Zuccotto – Ice cream cake
Panforte – Cake made in Siena with honey, cloves, candied fruits and almonds. Good to take home.
Castagnaccio – Cake made with chestnuts, pine nuts and sultanas
Torrone – Nougat

Late Night Snack
The Florentines love a late-night pasta dish washed down with Chianti wine, followed by 'biscotti di Prato' which are dipped in Vin Santo toscano, a sweet dessert wine used at the altar during Mass.

Tuscan Wines

A small hill area near Florence is called Chianti. It's from these hillsides that the renowned dry red Chianti wines are produced. Also try the other regional wines such as the dry red Rùfina, the white dry Vernaccia of St. Gimignano, the red and sweet Aleatico di Portoferraio, the dry red Brunello di Montalcino and the slightly bitter Nobile di Montepulciano.

For a sparkling wine, try Spumanti dell'Elba.

If you're hovering between production years, an oft-quoted rule of thumb is to choose the youngest white wines, and experiment with the oldest available red.

11.5 Restaurant suggestions

Price guideline

Prices in the listed restaurants may be subject to change; and obviously everyone orders differently. But here's the price grading system:

£	=	under £10
££	=	£10-£20
£££	=	£21-£25

Note: For street addresses, there are two numbering systems in Florence. Red are for businesses, and black for private houses. Thus, 96/r = 96 rosso (red), which will be nowhere near 96 'black'. Watch it!

Restaurants for special occasions

It is advisable with all these restaurants to make a phone reservation, to avoid disappointment.

La Loggia, Piazzale Michaelangelo
Tel: 2342832   £££
Dine outside on the terrace in the summer months.

Paoli, Via dei Tavolini   Tel: 216215
Old Florentine palace with frescoes & flowers. For 'special' treatment, speak to Benito the boss. Closed Tuesdays.   ££

La Posta, Via de'Lamberti   Tel: 212701
Just the place, if you like fish and a good selection
of desserts. Closed Tuesdays.   £££
Da Noi, Via Fiesolana   Tel: 242917
Intimate atmosphere. Friendly assistance given by
Sabina and Bruno. Booking essential. Closed
Sundays and Mondays.   £££
Il Bargello, Piazza della Signoria   Tel: 214071
Wholesome Tuscan cooking plus international fare.
Closed Mondays.   ££

Eating at reasonable prices

Guibbe Rosse, Piazza della Repubblica 13
Tel: 212280
Try their 'Scaloppine alla Chiantigiana' – a secret
recipe for escalope of veal in a Chianti based sauce.
Delicious! From May to October you can dine out-
doors.   ££
Trattoria Mossacce, 55 Via Proconsolo
Tel: 294361
A tourist menu on request. Closed Sundays.   £
Ristorante Spada, 62 Via della Spada
Tel: 218757
Menu available in English. Closed Sundays.   ££
Pizzeria/ristorante Vecchia Carlino
15/17 Via Fratelli Rosselli   Tel: 353678
Good selection of Tuscan food, and excellent pizzas
in the evenings. Closed Mondays.   ££
Da Nello, 56 Borgo Pinti   Tel: 2478410
Good selection of meat and fish.   ££
Yellow Bar, Via Proconsolo 39/r
Excellent pizza and pasta. Open evenings only.
Closed Tuesdays.   £
La Maremmana, Via Macci 77/r   Tel: 241226
Speciality Pasta alla Scoglio (Pasta with seafood).
Closed Sundays.   ££
Le Follie, Lugarno del Tempio 50   Tel: 677693
Pizzeria & Restaurant. Closed Tuesdays.   ££
La Burrasca, Via Panicale
Excellent Pasta.   ££
Diletto, Via Aretina 92/r   Tel: 678391
Closed Sunday.   £

Tuscan eating

Bibo, Piazza Felicita   Tel: 2398554
Good Tuscan food with excellent service and average prices. Closed Tuesdays.   ££

Osteria del Cinghiale Bianco   Tel: 215706
Borgo S. Jacopo 43/r
Tuscan specialities. Closed Wednesday.   ££

Leo in Santa Croce, 7 Via Torta   Tel: 210829
Try Leo's *crostoni*. Closed Sundays.   ££

La Barcaccia   Tel: 283958
corner of Via Verdi and Via Lavatoi.
Try the Fiorentina steak – one suffices for two persons. Closed Tuesdays.   ££

Il Latini, Via Palchetti 6/r   Tel: 210916
Go early, hungry as a lion. Closed Mondays.   ££

Armando, 140 Via Borgo Orgnissanti Tel: 216219
Very pleasant atmosphere besides good food. Closed Wednesdays.   ££

Il Profeta, 93/r Via Borgo Orgnissanti
Tel: 212265   ££
Excellent service and good food. Closed Sundays.

Osteria 'Da Quinto', Piazza Peruzzi 5   ££
Great atmosphere and good food. The proprietor may even sing for you!   Tel: 213323

Baldini Trattoria, Via il Prato 96/r   Tel: 287663
Closed Saturdays and Sundays.   ££

Cantinone del Gallo Nero
Via S. Spirito 6/r   Tel: 218898
Typical Tuscan food. Closed Mondays.   £

Trattoria Tito, Via San Gallo 112/r
Typical Tuscan trattoria. Closed Sundays.   £

L'Orologio, Piazza Ferrucci 5/r   Tel: 6811729
Good Tuscan food. Closed Sundays.   £

Light meals

Break, Via delle Terme
Try their *crostoni*. Open till midnight.
Closed Sun.   £

Le Belle Donne, Via delle Belle Donne
Good home-made food.
Closed Sundays.   ££

Vegetarian
Almanacco, Via Delle Route
Go early. Closed Sundays.   £

Fish restaurants
Trattoria Vittoria   Tel: 225757
52 Via Fonderia (corner Ponte Vittoria).
Closed Wednesdays.   £££

Pierot, 25 Piazza Gaddi   Tel: 702100
Closed Sundays.   ££

Note: In the above two restaurants, prices depend
upon which seafood you choose, as fresh fish is
sold by weight. Therefore check menu carefully
before ordering. Scampi, for example, are normally
priced per etto – about four ounces – *not* per
portion.

Chapter Twelve

Nightlife

Take to the streets! – A favourite pastime is strolling around the city-centre streets, enjoying the evening air and stopping for a drink, an ice cream, a meal or a chat. In the stretch between Piazza della Signoria and the Cathedral Square – especially along Via Calzaìuoli – is a complete summertime range of street entertainers.

See Florence lit-up – Take a bus up to Piazza Michelangelo, and admire the illuminated city across the river.

Dancing the night away – Although Florence is not one of the world's great nightlife centres, the city has some 20 discotheques and dance halls, plus a few open-air dancing venues during summer around the Viale Michelangelo and at Fiesole. They're mostly on the expensive side, so ask your local travel-agency representative for advice.

Classical Music – If you're in Florence during the May-July period, check on opera, ballet and concert programmes of the festival called Maggio Musicale Fiorentino. During summer months many open-air music performances are set in the courtyard of the Pitti Palace. July and August, at Fiesole, there's a season of concerts and films in the Roman theatre.

October and November is the main season for concerts at the Teatro Comunale (Corso Italia 16), with an opera season that usually runs from mid-December to mid-January.

Your tour rep can tell you what's on.

Chapter Thirteen

Italian art through the ages

The Etruscans (8th to 2nd centuries BC)

In pre-Roman and early-Roman times, a number of independent Etruscan city-states flourished in central Italy. Numerous archaeological sites have been identified mainly between the Rivers Arno and Tiber.

An important settlement was at Fiesole, just outside present-day Florence. The Etruscans were maritime traders in frequent contact with the Greeks further south. In their artwork they were greatly influenced by the Greeks.

Etruscan power waned from the 5th century BC, while Rome gradually expanded throughout the region and assimilated the Etruscan culture. In effect, Etruscan history dissolved into that of Rome. Great quantities of artefacts have come from excavations especially within the necropolis sites of the principal Etruscan cities, including Fiesole.

Italy's richest collection of Etruscan art was originally formed by the Medici dynasty, and is housed in the Archaeological Museum in Via della Colonna.

Roman times (753 BC to 5th century AD)

During their rise and expansion the Romans left their mark throughout Italy, the Mediterranean, Middle East and north to the borders of Scotland. They developed Fiesole into a major town with a forum, temple, capitol, baths and a 3,000-seat theatre.

Later they established a military colony to guard their strategic bridge at Florence.

While the Romans shone as colonisers, military men, administrators and engineers, they mainly relied on the Greeks to set the patterns for art and architecture. In their construction of bridges, aqueducts, basilicas and other public buildings, the Romans mastered the use of concrete and brick, along with the new technology of the arch. Greek temple-building aesthetics and Roman know-how were combined into monuments which still arouse awed respect 19 centuries' later.

The Greeks also contributed their artistic flair with statuary, which was copied in disciplined style by Roman craftsmen.

Early Middle Ages (4th-11th centuries)

With the triumph of Christianity as the official religion in the 4th century, Roman basilicas were converted into churches. New church building followed the basic theme of a long hall with two aisles and a semi-circular apse at the far end. Decorative themes were imported from Constantinople – the original Byzantium, capital of the Eastern Roman Empire.

Romanesque (11th-12th centuries)

During this period of European stability and prosperity there was a great wave of church building in all the Italian cities. The intense activity led to much innovation in architectural techniques and styles, while artists began to create highly individual works of pictorial and sculptural decoration.

The word 'Romanesque' originally stood for architecture 'in the Roman style', especially in the use of the rounded arch and barrel vaulting. Churches kept mostly to the earlier Christian basilica form with a three-aisled nave, a transcept and a semi-circular apse roofed by a half-dome.

Most of the Italian churches of the period stayed with the tradition of wooden ceilings or open rafters. In Tuscany, the Romanesque style retained many traditional architectural details such as the crowning of marble columns with classical Roman capitals. Sculpture was confined mainly to reliefs. The most important Italian centre for sculpture at this time was the Lombardy region in the north.

Interior church decoration was almost entirely in the form of frescoes, following traditions that were well established from Roman and early Christian times.

Gothic (12th-14th centuries)

A new outlook came through the teachings of St Francis of Assissi (1182-1226) who preached a more gentle and lovable religion in contrast to the former stern austerity. Painters broke loose from the formal conventions of the Byzantine School, with Giotto in Florence leading the way to a fresh and life-like style.

In place of the austere Byzantine backgrounds, biblical stories were set in contemporary dress amid local scenery with the familiar hills and countryside of Tuscany. Easel painting came into more general use around this time, permitting a more subtle expression of deep emotions.

Meanwhile, Italian gothic monuments provided large wall and ceiling areas for mural decoration. During this period, the principal technique of fresco painting was based on wet plaster – just enough being applied to a working surface that could be finished in a single day's session. Painters had to work fast, before the plaster dried out. Compositions were mapped out in red chalk. Filling in the details was a team effort, with the master craftsman directing the operation.

Among the great names in this technique were Giotto, Taddeo Gaddi and Maso di Banco in Florence, and Pietro Cavallini in Rome.

Renaissance (15th-16th centuries)

The Renaissance or cultural 'rebirth' of the 15th and 16th centuries marked the end of the Middle Ages, with a revolution in thought that rediscovered the creative heritage of classical Greek and Roman philosophy, literature and science. The revived interest in the classical world opened up new art themes based on Greek and Roman history and mythology. Artists themselves emerged as imaginative creators rather than as mere craftsmen. In the artistic and cultural history of Western Europe, the Renaissance had the deepest possible influence.

Although Giotto was an isolated forerunner, Early Renaissance developed from a generation of artists who worked in Florence at the start of the 15th century. The trend-setters were Donatello for sculpture, Brunelleschi for architecture and Massachio for painting – later followed in mid-century by Botticelli in Florence and Giovanni Bellini in Venice.

Florence remained the centre of innovation throughout the 15th century, but other schools followed similar lines, especially in Milan, Venice, Padua and Naples.

In a supremely productive period, about 1495-1520, a few artists of great genius – Leonardo da Vinci, Michelangelo, Bramante, Raphael and Titian – brought a High Renaissance style to perfection. Five centuries later, their works are part of the heritage of modern man.

Masters of the Italian School

The word 'school' has nothing to do with teaching! It is applied to the artists of different nations, and of groups of painters within one nation. Italian School – a label mainly applied to the Renaissance artists – is sub-divided into regional schools which each had its individual character, reflecting the local environment and taste of the time. Art experts distinguish between about twenty schools of Italian painting, of which Florence, Venice and Siena are among the most important.

Obviously there was an overlap of styles and techniques, especially when artists moved from the patronage of one city to another. But part of the pleasure of looking at Italian paintings comes from recognising this variety between the regional schools.

As the Church was the single most important patron, religious art predominated. Until the late 13th century, Italian art was influenced mainly by Byzantine techniques of working with mosaic. Artworks depicted rather stiff and gloomy characters in the story of Jesus against a formal gold background.

Fresco painting flourished, to reach its perfection during the early 16th century in the hands of Raphael and Michelangelo. Oil painting – invented about 1500 – then took over in popularity.

In general, the Florentines preferred a soft tenderness in their paintings, compared with the raw vigour of the Venetians. In the use of colour, the Florentine School inclined towards a cooler approach – rose and purple blue compared with the Venetian leaning towards opulent orange.

Late Renaissance and Mannerism (16th-17th centuries)

The sack of Rome in 1527 by the German and Spanish troops of Holy Roman Emperor Charles V marked the temporary end of Papal patronage. Many leading artists moved to other centres in Italy, Spain and France. Meanwhile, in this Late Renaissance period, a new style called Mannerism had evolved, characterised by highly refined grace and elegance.

This was the age of Palladio and Caravaggio, Cellini, Tintoretto and Veronese, whose prolific works are found throughout North and Central Italy.

Baroque (17th-18th centuries)

By the end of the 16th century, Mannerism had run its course, to be superseded by the highly ornate Baroque style. Caravaggio set the trend in painting, Bernini in sculpture and Borromini in architecture. Baroque was introduced to northern Europe mainly through Rubens, who had studied in Italy during the formative period of 1600-1608. But the main centre of Baroque for most of the 17th century was Rome.

The spectacular style became highly popular throughout the Catholic world, and also among monarchs and other wealthy secular patrons. The style survived into the 18th century, to be replaced in turn by Rococo. Among the leading artists of the period were Bernini, Canaletto, Guardi and Tiepolo. With their passing, the greatest days of Italian painting came to an end.

Chapter Fourteen

Who's Who in Art and Myth

14.1 The principal artists
Here are some brief notes on some of the leading artists whose work can be seen in Florence, or who influenced the development of Florentine art.

Botticelli – 1445-1510. A highly influential painter of the Early Renaissance, Sandro Botticelli was initially apprenticed to a Florentine goldsmith but then switched to painting under the guidance of Fra Filippo Lippi. He also had links with the painter and sculptor Verrocchio, in whose studio Leonardo da Vinci was an apprentice. The Uffizi Gallery contains a rich collection of many of his early paintings, including those commissioned by the Medici family. In 1481 Pope Sixtus IV commissioned him to help decorate the side walls of the newly completed Sistine Chapel.

The following ten years represented the peak of Botticelli's career, with his workshop producing a wide variety of pictures. The expulsion of his Medici patrons from Florence in 1494 was a major blow to his career. Leonardo's return to Florence in 1501 helped establish new trends, and Botticelli subsequently did little work until he died impoverished. But his influence remained into the next generation, especially through his pupil, Filippino Lippi – the son of his own teacher.

Brunelleschi – 1377-1446. A leading architect of the early Renaissance, Filippo Brunelleschi lost the contract for the Baptistery bronze doors in competition with Ghiberti. But his career was crowned by his work on building the dome on Florence cathedral – a project which had been left unfinished in the 14th century because of apparently insoluble structural problems.

He left his mark on numerous other buildings of the time, and was a major influence on his successors, including Michelangelo and Donato Bramante. He is credited with new techniques of perspective painting, used in subsequent Renaissance art.

Cellini – 1500-1571. A typical 'Renaissance man', Benvenuto Cellini was equally versatile as a writer, sculptor, goldsmith or architect. Born in Florence, he learned his gold-working skills from his father, who doubled as a musician.

In his early years – between 1516 and 1540 – Cellini moved around the principal cities of Italy, working for the papacy and for aristocratic patrons. From 1540 he spent several years on commissions for the French court at Fonatainebleau. He then returned to Florence in 1545, into the service of Cosimo Medici. Cellini's most famous work in Florence is the statue of Perseus with the head of Medusa in the Loggia dei Lanzi which faces onto the Piazza della Signoria. The Bargello Museum has more of his work.

Cimabue – 1240-1302. A Florentine painter whose style marked a transition from the Byzantine roots of Christian art to the new direction of the Early Renaissance. That link came through his pupil, Giotto. Regrettably one of Cimabue's finest paintings – *Crucifix* in Santa Croce – was virtually destroyed in the River Arno flood of 1966. The Uffizi gallery has a very large wooden panel of *Madonna and Christ Child Enthroned*; and there are mosaics in Pisa Cathedral.

Donatello – 1386-1466. As a contemporary of Ghiberti, Donatello was a front runner among Florentine sculptors of the early Renaissance. He covered every medium of sculpture, lively and full of character. His figures reflected the personality and inner life of his subjects. His work is easiest seen in the Donatello room at the Bargello in Florence, where the highlight is his statue of *David*. This was the first free-standing bronze nude since classical times, and reflects the Renaissance admiration of physical beauty.

Fra Filippo Lippi – 1406-1469. He began life as a painter monk in a Carmelite monastery, but later ran off with a nun and had an illegitimate child. He made his mark among Florentine painters of the Early Renaissance, as a fine draftsman who could bring biblical stories to vivid and colourful life. His mistress posed as the Madonna in Room 8 of the Uffizi. His pupils included Botticelli and his own son, Filippino Lippi (see below).

Gaddi – A three-generation family of painters who were eminent in Florence for over 100 years. Gaddo Gaddi (1250-1330) was a contemporary of Giotto. Gaddo's son, Taddeo (1300-1366), was a talented pupil and collaborator of Giotto, whose influence is apparent in the *Life of the Virgin* fresco in Santa Croce. Taddeo's son Agnolo (c. 1350-1396) followed the same Giotto tradition with frescoes in the choir of Santa Croce. Another son turned to banking and laid the basis of a considerable family fortune

Ghiberti – 1378-1455. Lorenzo Ghiberti was born in Florence, where he spent his working life as a greatly admired Renaissance sculptor who initially learned his metal-working skill from his goldsmith stepfather. As a true Renaissance man, he was a close student of nature and of the classical tradition, and also worked as a painter. A writer on art subjects, he produced the earliest surviving autobiography of a working artist. His greatest work is the remarkable *Gates of Paradise* – the bronze doors to the Baptistery, facing the Duomo.

Giorgione – 1477-1510. As a talented Venetian poet, musician and painter, Giorgione played a key role in the early 16th-century shift to High Renaissance style. In his brief career (cut short by the

Plague), he initially worked as a pupil of the Bellini brothers, but then began to absorb some of the techniques of Leonardo da Vinci. Several paintings attributed to Giorgione were completed by his contemporary, Titian, who was greatly influenced by Giorgione's innovations, which Titian developed during his long life.

Giotto – 1266-1337 – was the great pioneer of Renaissance art, in Florence, where some of his finest work is found. As a 10-year-old shepherd boy he was 'discovered' by Cimabue, who trained him in his studio.

In Florence, examples of Giotto's work can be seen in Santa Croce, in the Bardi and Peruzzi chapels. He had no architectural training, but laid out the initial design of the Duomo.

Leonardo da Vinci – 1452-1519. Born near Florence, he showed artistic talent from an early age, and was apprenticed to the workshop of a leading Renaissance master named Andrea Verrocchio. Leonardo entered the painters' guild in 1472, and his earliest masterworks date from then.

From 1482, for an 18-year period, Leonardo worked for the ruling Sforza family of Milan – producing court portraits, arranging festivals, designing military fortifications and painting *The Last Supper*. During that period he undertook wide-ranging scientific and technical studies in anatomy, biology, map-making, mathematics and physics.

From 1500 he spent time in Venice, Florence and Rome before returning again to Milan; then, in 1513, back to Rome for a three-year stint, mainly devoted to theoretical research. His last years were spent in France, as architectural consultant to the French king. Leonardo must rate as the most creative mind of the age – a true Renaissance man.

Lippi, Filippino – 1457-1504. A son and pupil of his painter father, he later studied under Botticelli. In 1484 he completed the Masaccio frescoes in the Brancacci Chapel. From 1488 onwards he painted many important frescoes both in Rome and Florence

– in the Strozzi Chapel of Santa Maria Novella, for instance.

Masaccio – 1401-1428. Despite his early death, Masaccio rates as one of the co-founders of the Florentine Renaissance. Greatly influenced by Giotto, he also learned about perspective from Brunelleschi, and dramatization of the human figure from Donatello. His pioneer use of perspective in fresco painting can be seen in the church of Santa Maria Novella. The use of light and shadow techniques – called *chiaroscuro* – is shown dramatically in his frescoes in the Brancacci Chapel of Santa Maria del Carmine.

Michelangelo – 1475-1564. Greatest of the Renaissance artists, Michelangelo was a giant in painting, sculpture and architecture. His origins were Florentine, and from the age of 13 he was trained by the painter Ghirlandaio and the sculptor Bertoldo di Giovanni. In adolescence he came under the wing of the Medici family, giving him access to the leading intellectuals of the day. He rapidly made his mark with marble statues carved while in his twenties, including the *Pietà* in St Peter's, Rome, and the colossal marble *David* in the Accademia, Florence.

Called to Rome in 1505 to undertake a sculpture contract – a stupendous tomb for Pope Julius II – he was sidetracked into the even bigger assignment of portraying the biblical history of humanity on the Sistine Chapel ceiling. That four-year project (1508-1512) must rate as the greatest achievement of the High Renaissance style, changing the entire course of Western art.

In later years his outlook and his style changed. The artistic ferment is exemplified by his architectural and sculptural work on the Medici Chapel in Florence (1519-34), and in his *Last Judgement* in the Sistine Chapel (1536-41). In the final years of his long life, Michelangelo returned to his first love, sculpture. In 1550 he carved the *Pietà* in Florence Cathedral – a work which he intended to be sited over his own tomb. He died aged 88.

Perugino – 1445-1523. This eminent Renaissance painter probably trained in Florence where a number of his works are located. In 1481 he was leader of the project to decorate the walls of the Sistine Chapel, together with Botticelli and Ghirlandaio. His *Christ Giving the Keys to St Peter* survives, though his frescoes on the end wall were replaced by Michelangelo's *Last Judgement*. In his later years Perugino's large workshop of students and assistants included Raphael.

Raphael – 1483-1520. Among the greatest painters of the High Renaissance, Raphael started young, apprenticed at age 11 to the painter Perugino. By the age of 20 he was producing great masterpieces. Living in Florence from 1504 to 1508, he absorbed much from Leonardo da Vinci and other masters. Many examples of this highly productive period are treasured in the world's leading galleries.

At age 25 he was commissioned by Pope Julius II to supervise the decoration of the State Rooms in the Vatican Palace. Simultaneously Raphael produced paintings for many private patrons. In 1514 he was employed as chief architect of St Peter's Basilica. Although these designs never came to fruition, other architectural work in Rome and Florence still survives.

Uccello – 1397-1497. An extraordinary painter who was preoccupied with the mechanics of perspective. See his equestrian fresco of the English mercenary Sir John Hawkwood in Florence Cathedral, a battle scene in the Uffizi, and frescoes of *The Flood* in the Green Cloister of Santa Maria Novella.

Vasari - 1511-1574. Florentine author, painter and architect, Vasari produced a complete history of the Italian Renaissance through his detailed biographies of the principal artists. This pioneer work put forth the novel idea that artists were creative intellectuals rather than mere craftsmen who decorated walls and ceilings.

As an architect he designed the Uffizi for his patron, Cosimo I; also the high-level corridor above the Ponte Vecchio, and some additions to the Palazzo Vecchio, which he also decorated with frescoes.

Verrocchio – 1435-1488. A leading Florentine sculptor of the Early Renaissance. Initially a goldsmith, he made a smooth transition to monumental works of sculpture, and succeeded Donatello as the favourite sculptor of the Medici family. The bronze *David* in the Bargello is typical of his style. Among the pupils and assistants who trained in his workshop were Leonardo da Vinci and probably Perugino.

14.2 Who's who among the gods

From the Renaissance onwards, artists turned more frequently to subjects based on classical Roman mythology, which often had been adapted from the pantheon of the Greeks. Here's a short list of the more popular characters.

Apollo – or Phoebus, the sun god; the god of prophesy, music, song and the arts. Protector of flocks and herds.

Bacchus – Dionysos – god of vegetation, and the fruits of the trees, especially wine.

Cupid – the Greek Eros – the lovers' favourite.

Diana – otherwise known as Artemis – deity of the chase; goddess of the moon, protectress of the young. Sister of Apollo.

Fortuna – the Greek Tyche – personifying fortune, usually depicted holding a rudder, or with a globe or cornucopia.

Juno – Hera among the Greeks – the good wife of Jupiter.

Jupiter – Zeus – greatest of the Olympian Gods; father of both gods and men.

Mars – father of the twin founders of Rome, he was a Roman favourite with several temples to his name.

Medusa – one of the three Gorgon sisters – lost her head to Perseus, blood everywhere.

Mercury – Hermes – messenger of the gods, who usually wore a travelling hat, golden sandals, and a purse. Mercury was patron of merchants, thieves, artists, orators and travellers.

Minerva – based on the Greek Athena, goddess of war and wisdom; patroness of agriculture, industry and the arts.

Nemesis – the fatal divinity, measuring out happiness and unhappiness.

Neptune – Poseidon – god of the sea, and responsible for earthquakes.

Venus – otherwise known as Aphrodite – goddess of love and beauty; the Marilyn Monroe of classical times. Sometimes appears with a sea-horse or dolphin. Julius Caesar claimed her as an ancestor.

Chapter Fifteen

Travel hints

15.1 Money and banking

The Italian unit of currency is the lira (plural lire).

Coins	Notes
50 lire	1,000 lire
100 lire	2,000 lire
200 lire	5,000 lire
500 lire	10,000 lire
	50,000 lire
	100,000 lire

The symbol used for marking prices is either a letter 'L', or similar to the pound sterling sign – £.

Unless you're very fast at mental arithmetic, Italian lire are confusing for the first day or two. unless it's a handy equivalent like 2,500 lire to the pound. Suggestion: before departure, check the current exchange rate, and list out some conversions on a postcard, as a handy crib.

There is often a shortage of small change, and telephone tokens (worth 200 lire), sweets or stamps may be used to make up the deficiency.

Changing Money

Take a starter kit of a bundle of lire, to tide you over the first day or two in Italy, especially if you arrive at weekends. You can change money and cheques at the arrival airport or railway terminus. Banks are normally open 8.30 a.m. till 1.20 p.m., and for a variable hour in the afternoon, Monday till Friday, closed weekends. Rates vary from bank to bank, so it's worth comparing their display panels. A flat commission charge of up to 3000 lire on Traveller Cheques makes it uneconomic to change little and often. Some Exchange Bureaux keep longer hours, and take a bigger slice of your money. Larger hotels can also oblige, but give even more unfriendly rates.

Remember to take your passport when changing money.

Personal Cheques & Eurocheques

Backed by the appropriate banker's card, Eurocheques are among the simplest and most acceptable means of payment. These must be specially ordered from your bank, but are well worth it, as you can then write cheques in the local currency. They can also be used in UK.

The Eurocheque card allows you to cash up to £120 on each cheque, and is valid for making payments to shops, hotels and restaurants that display the 'ec' sign.

Many places also accept normal cheques up to £50 if backed by a banker's card.

Credit Cards

Access, Visa, American Express and Diners Club are widely accepted at shops and restaurants. At some banks you can withdraw cash, but it's often inconvenient. Don't over-rely on credit cards for getting cash, though automatic cash machines are becoming more prevalent.

The following banks accept major credit cards:

Banca d'America e d'Italia   Tel: 27 81 11
Via Strozzi (near Piazza della Repubblica)
   and at Via Por Santa Maria
Cassa di Risparmio di Firenze   Tel: 27 80 1
Via Maurizio Bufalini 4/6
Banco di Roma
Via dei Vecchietti
Credito Italiano   Tel: 27 97
Via dei Vecchietti II
Open: Monday-Thursday 8.20-13.20 and 14.45-15.45 hrs; Fridays 8.20-13.20 and 14.30-15.30 hrs. Closed on Saturdays and Sundays.

Exchange Bureau open late
Thomas Cook, 6R Lungano Acciaioli Tel: 289781
Open: Daily 9-19 hrs year-round.

Reconverting cash
In general, convert any surplus lire back into sterling or dollars at the departure airport. Avoid taking 50,000 and 100,000 lire notes back into the UK, as banks may refuse to change them and certainly will give a lower rate.

15.2 Security
Pickpockets
Just like in any other European country, Italy's main cities have their quota of hardworking pickpockets who specialise in the tourist traffic. Their guess is that holidaymaker handbags or wallets will contain an above-average supply of currency, traveller cheques and credit cards. The light-fingered gentry are not necessarily bent Italians. International teams are also at work during the season, often looking just like other tourists.

Be particularly careful in crowded places, or when travelling by bus. Pickpockets frequently work in pairs, taking advantage of crowds to jostle or distract their victims while stealing a purse or wallet. In narrow side-streets, skilled riders on scooters have perfected a motorised bag-snatching technique as they swoop past.

There's no need to be suspicious of all strangers. But don't make things easy for crooks.

Never carry a wallet in your hip pocket. Keep handbags fastened and held securely. In a café or restaurant, don't hang camera or handbag over the back of your chair.

Minimise any potential loss by leaving the bulk of your valuables in the safety deposits available to hotel guests. Keep a separate record of traveller-cheque numbers, and also of credit-card details of where to notify in case of loss.

If you have anything stolen, report the theft to the nearest police station and obtain an official declaration of theft, required for insurance reclaim.

If you're on a package tour with insurance cover, contact the travel-agency representative for advice on making a 'Loss Report' to send with your claim form. The address in Florence is: Questura, Via Zara 2. Tel: 49771.

If your passport has gone missing, once you have the police report you should go to the British Consulate at Lungarno Corsini 2 (Tel: 284133), taking two passport size photographs. The Consulate will issue a temporary passport to get you home.

Female harrassment

Of course, it does exist. Best advice is to ignore the persistent overtures, until the young idiots get tired of the game and try elsewhere. Otherwise, say "NO!" in loud English. It means the same in Italian. You could also respond in basic Anglo-Saxon, which would be equally well understood.

15.3 Postal and phone services

Post Offices (Ufficio Postale) handle telegrams, mail and money transfers, and some have public telephones. Opening hours are generally Mon-Fri 8.15-14.00 hours. The system gets low marks for efficiency, and queues are long. Air mail seems to travel by slow pigeon, and you'll easily race post-cards home.

The **Central Post Office** is located at Via Pietrapiana. Open: 9-13 hrs Mon-Sat.

The Post Office at Via Pellicceria is open 8.30-19.00 hrs.

Stamps are also sold at tobacconists' (tabaccheria) with a 'T' sign above the door. They're a lot more helpful if you buy some postcards at the same time! Likewise, some hotel desks carry a stamp supply. Stamps are 'francobolli' in Italian.

Post boxes are red, and non-local mail should be posted in the slot marked 'altre destinazioni'.

Phoning home

Making long distance and international calls from hotels is an expensive luxury! Instead, go to the nearest office of S.I.P. (pronounced *seep*) – short for Società Italiana Posta/Telefoni. There's a line of cabins, and a queue. When your turn comes, the counter clerk will tell you which booth number to use.

(1) Dial 00 for International Exchange, and wait for a tone change.

(2) Dial 44 (the international code for UK) plus the appropriate STD town dialling code, minus the first zero; then the local number. Thus, to call Barnsley (code 0226) 12345, dial 0044 226 12345. Other country codes are: USA and Canada 1; Australia 61; New Zealand 64; Eire 353.

(3) Afterwards, you return to the desk to pay for the telephone call at the regular cost with no mark-ups. Calls are cheaper after 11 p.m. or before 8 a.m., and throughout the weekend from 14.30 hrs on Saturday.

International Telephone Offices are located at Via Cavour 21 (Centro Telefonici Pubblici S.I.P.) and at the Post Offices in Via Pellicceria, Via Pietrapiana and at the Railway Station.

The Post Office in Via Pellicceria is open for telephone calls 24 hours a day, seven days a week. Use the bell outside the main entrance if the doors are shut.

At the Railway Station, the S.I.P. Office is open 7.30-21.30 hrs daily.

Phone cards called *scheda*, costing 5,000 or 10,000 lire at S.I.P. offices and tobacconists, are a handy way of making international phone calls. Slide the card into the call box, and the residual value shows on the screen. Long distance calls can be made from telephone boxes with a yellow disc and the word 'teleselezione' or 'interurbana'.

Coin boxes: For local calls, you'll need two 100-lire coins or one 200-lire coin for the modern call box; or occasionally a *gettone* (token) which costs 200 lire at a bar.

Lift receiver, dial, and insert the token when the connection is made. 'Guasto' means broken or out of order.

Reverse charge calls to UK or North America can be placed by inserting your basic 200 lire, and dialling 172 followed by the national code. You then negotiate your reverse-charge number with the operator in the home country. If you come equipped with a British Telecom chargecard – or AT&T for North America – the cost can be charged direct to your home number.

To call Florence from other countries, the international code is 39-55. Thus, from Britain, dial 010-39-55 followed by the local number in Florence. From North America, dial 011-39-55 etc.

15.4 Medical

As part of EEC reciprocal health arrangements, UK visitors can get all medical services that are available to Italians. Before departure from Britain, ask your local Department of Health and Social Security (DHSS) office for the "Medical Costs Abroad" leaflet no. SA30. Fill out the form CM1 and send it to the DHSS, who will supply form E111 to take with you. It's probably not worth the effort for minor ailments, but would be most useful if anything major happened.

Should you require a doctor, contact your hotel concierge and ask him to call one.

If you have holiday or medical insurance, get receipts both from the doctor and the chemist, so as to make any necessary reclaim. If you're on a package tour, and sizeable funds are needed to cover medical expenses, contact your travel-agency rep for advice.

If mosquitoes normally have you for supper, bring some repellent. Biting insects are most active in July and August. To ensure peaceful sleep, you can outwit night-flying insects by keeping bedroom windows closed and air conditioning switched on. It's also worth packing an electrically-operated mosquito kit, which can be remarkably effective.

A combination of hot weather, iced drinks and different food can cause tummy problems. If the bug hits, doctors advise drinking plenty of fruit juice - such as lemon or orange - or bottled water with a twitch of sugar and salt (to counter dehydration). Continue eating normally. Among the pharmaceuticals, Lomotil, Imodium and Arrêt are usually effective, and one of those may be worth packing. Local doctors can provide stronger preparations if necessary.

You have to be desperate, to use the facilities in some of the wayside cafés which you may wish to visit in a hurry. Sometimes the gap between utter misery and fulfillment is measured by a few sheets of toilet paper. Always carry a few spares in your holdall, in case of emergencies.

Chemists are open only during normal shop hours, but a window sign indicates the nearest night or Sunday-opening chemist ('farmacia').

15.5 *What to wear and pack*

Casual dress is OK for tourist Florence, though you may prefer something more formal for any up-market evening dining or a visit to a musical evening. Most likely you'll be on your feet most of the day, so forget about high heels. Comfortable flat footwear is much better.

To enter the Cathedral and many other churches in Florence you should be soberly dressed: no shorts; no above-the-knee skirts; no sleeveless dresses (though women can get by with a scarf draped over shoulders). Otherwise you will be politely turned away.

If you want to use any electric gadgets, pack a plug adaptor. Florence is on 220 volts, but uses the Continental-type 2-pin plug.

Don't worry if your cosmetic, pharmaceutical or film supplies run out. All the major brands are readily available.

However, take somewhat more camera film than you normally carry to other destinations. Although Florence is not so high in photo subjects as Venice or Rome, why waste precious time buying more film on the spot, at prices that are higher than back home?

In the expectation of buying some stylish Florentine clothing, many visitors travel out light in their luggage to leave room for the loot.

Chapter Sixteen

Further reference

16.1 Public holidays

1 January	New Year's Day
6 January	Epiphany
25 April	Liberation Day, 1945
Easter Monday	
1 May	May Day
15 August	Assumption
1 November	All Saints
8 December	Immaculate Conception
25 December	Christmas Day
26 December	St Stephen's Day

Be prepared for 3-day closure of banking and other services when any of these holidays makes a bridge with the weekend.

16.2 Whom to contact

Emergency

Police – Fire Brigade – Ambulance –   Dial 113
Medical (Holidays, Night – doctor on call) 477891
Ambulance, First Aid   212222
English Chemist, Via Tornabuoni 97
Chemists Open 24 hours a day:
Communale 13 – inside the main railway station
Molteni – Via dei Calzaiuoli 7r   Tel: 263490
Taverna – Piazza San Giovanni 20r   Tel: 211343

Night Chemists (open 20.00 hrs to 08.30 hrs):
Codeca – Via de' Ginori 50   Tel: 270849
San Giovanni di Dio – Borgo Ognissanti 40r
Pagliacci – Via della Scala 49r   Tel: 275612

Lost Property

Stolen passports & money should be reported to the Carabinieri (police HQ) at Borgo Ognissanti 48. A police report, made within 24 hours of the loss, is necessary for any insurance reclaim.

City Council Lost Property Office – Via Circondaria 19.

Losses on trains – Lost Property Office inside the central railway station, by platform 1.

Consulates

British – Lungarno Corsini 2   Tel: 284133
US – Lungarno Amerigo Vespucci 38 Tel: 298276

16.3 Tourist offices

For information in Florence, contact:
Azienda Autonoma di Turismo di Firenze
    Via de Tornabuoni 15   Tel: 678841
Mon-Sat 9-13 hrs for city maps, brochures etc.
Ente Provinciale per il Turismo (EPT) Tel: 678841
    Via Manzoni 16 – information about Tuscany.

More Information

For more information before you travel, contact the Italian State Tourist Office (ENIT for short):

London – 1 Princes Street, London W1R 8AY. Tel: (071) 408-1254. Mon-Fri 9-14.30 hrs.

Dublin – 47 Merrion Sq., Dublin 2. Tel: 766397.

New York – 630 Fifth Avenue, Suite 1565, New York, NY 10111. Tel: (212) 245-4822/4.

Chicago – 500 North Michigan Avenue, Chicago, IL 60611. Tel: (312) 644-0990/1.

San Francisco – 360 Post Street, Suite 801, San Francisco, CA 94109. Tel: (415) 392-6206/7.

Montreal – Store 56, Plaza 3, Place Ville-Marie, Montreal, Quebec. Tel: (514) 866-7667.

Sydney – c/o Alitalia, AGC House, 124 Philip Street, Sydney, NSW 2000. Tel: (2) 22-13-620.

Auckland – c/o Alitalia, 95 Queen Street, Auckland. Tel: (9) 79-44-55.

Johannesburg – London House, 21 Loveday Street, Johannesburg 2000 (Box 6507). Tel: 83-83-247.